An OPUS book

METAPHYSICS

OPUS General Editors

Keith Thomas
Alan Ryan
Walter Bodmer

OPUS books provide concise, original, and authoritative introductions to a wide range of subjects in the humanities and sciences. They are written by experts for the general reader as well as for students.

Metaphysics

The Logical Approach

JOSÉ A. BENARDETE

Oxford   New York

OXFORD UNIVERSITY PRESS

1989

Oxford University Press, Walton Street, Oxford ox2 6DP

Oxford New York Toronto
Delhi Bombay Calcutta Madras Karachi
Petaling Jaya Singapore Hong Kong Tokyo
Nairobi Dar es Salaam Cape Town
Melbourne Auckland

and associated companies in
Berlin Ibadan

Oxford is a trade mark of Oxford University Press

First published 1989 as an Oxford University Press paperback
and simultaneously in a hardback edition

British Library Cataloguing in Publication Data

Benardete, José A.
Metaphysics : the logical approach.—(OPUS).
1. Metaphysics
I. Title II. Series
110
ISBN 0-19-219217-5
ISBN 0-19-289203-7 Pbk.

Library of Congress Cataloging in Publication Data

Benardete, José A. (José Amado)
Metaphysics : the logical approach / José A. Benardete.
p. cm.—(An OPUS book)
Bibliography: p. Includes index.
1. Metaphysics. I. Title. II. Series: OPUS.
110—dc19 BD111.B39 88-9933
1989
ISBN 0-19-219217-5
ISBN 0-19-289203-7 (pbk.)

Typeset by Colset Pte Ltd.
Printed in Great Britain by
Biddles Ltd.
Guildford and King's Lynn

To Catherine Lord

Let us not fail to notice that there is a difference between arguments from and those to the first principles. For Plato, too, was right in raising this question and asking, as he used to do, 'Are we on the way from or to the first principles?'

ARISTOTLE

Contents

Introduction

Launching metaphysics as a systematic enterprise, Aristotle is soon seen to be defining it twice over, once in fairly technical terms and again in an almost ostentatiously vernacular fashion. Technically defined as the theory of being *qua* being, metaphysics is more accommodatingly summed up by Aristotle in a single word: wisdom. How these two definitions connect with one another remains a source of puzzlement to the present day.

Although some notion of wisdom, however inchoate, may be presumed to be available to human beings everywhere, even to the most primitive, there is a tendency to relegate its actual possession to remote ancestors, if not to the gods. At any rate, this is proposed as a cross-cultural hypothesis which professional anthropologists are invited to investigate. But metaphysics aside, how shall wisdom be defined, if only for the purpose of that investigation? Readily enough, as an understanding of the deepest or most fundamental things. That it should be philosophy and not, say, poetry (recalling Plato's attack on the poets) that is called on for such understanding, one has every right to query. Moreover, there have always been students of philosophy who, even after prolonged immersion in the subject, have despaired of achieving wisdom in the absence of some divine revelation. It is with some such thought in mind that Aristotle expresses the fear that his launching of metaphysics may expose him to the charge of impiety, on the ground that the gods may be expected to reserve wisdom to themselves, out of jealousy. In less personal terms, this almost Old Testament jealousy may be presumed to reflect the following line of argument. What distinguishes God from anything else must be the best of things; wisdom and not, say, immortality is the best of things, therefore. . . . Smacking of impiety at the outset, metaphysics comes to be viewed anew in the age of modern science as a presumptuous, if not pretentious, undertaking, as, in three successive waves, Hume, Kant, and Wittgenstein proceed to subject its cognitive credentials to the most searching critique, the end result after only a few years, the smoke having cleared, being its re-emergence today as a safe, scholastic discipline in which, however, only specialists take any great interest. Tucked away in an obscure niche of the university, it is only to be expected that metaphysical researchers should hesitate to advertise themselves as the custodians of wisdom, not least because their professional colleagues in other departments would take offence at the suggestion.

In particular, the claim that it is metaphysics, not physics, that addresses the fundamental things is not one to which the scientific community is likely to assent; in fact, at the outset of his enquiry, Aristotle enthusiastically endorses the prima-facie plausibility of its being physics that engages the deepest things. As the word itself indicates, 'metaphysics' is defined by way of express contrast with physics, *beyond* which it fixes its sight, there is reason to believe that metaphysics as a systematic undertaking is launched by Aristotle under the auspices of a critique of physical inquiry informed by the new science of logic, which he also instituted. This emergence of logic and metaphysics in tandem, not remarked upon by Aristotle himself, has only come to be appreciated in recent years.

Basic to Aristotle's logic, if not to (just about) all subsequent logic, is the grammatical distinction between subject and predicate, which the philosopher comes to gloss in terms of the contrast between a substance and its properties. It is that contrast, above all, that provides the slender patrimony off which, in one form or another, metaphysics continues to live to the present day; thus, even so simple a sentence as 'Socrates is snub-nosed' is felt to involve predicating snub-nosedness of Socrates. Classified by the grammarian as an abstract singular term, the neologism 'snub-nosedness' appears to designate something (possessed in common by all snub-nosed people) of which the man in the street can be supposed to be at best only dimly aware. Whether such recherché items credited largely to Plato should rather be scorned as the merest artefacts of philosophical jargon that answer to nothing in reality, remains a question that one persists in cherishing as the archetypal theme of metaphysics. *How* a property might belong to a thing—whether essentially or accidentally—is one sort of complication, which supplies the theme of Chapter 1. A further complication, namely, how a property might belong to a thing—whether relatively or absolutely speaking—is the topic of Chapter 2. The rest of the book is simply more of the same, as I back and fill, veer and tack, in an extended meta-physical investigation that, in the end, will be seen to feature essence and the absolute.

These two themes prompt reflections of a more systematic sort in Chapter 3, where their precise role in the theory of being *qua* being is defined. Chapter 4 focuses on Hegel, whose conception of metaphysics as the rational reconstruction of formal logic will be seen to connect with Frege on a nuts-and-bolts level. A professional mathematician, Frege is acclaimed for having revolutionized the entire science of logic at a single blow in 1879; but philosophers have been extraordinarily slow in bringing that revolution specifically to bear on the metaphysical agenda as bequeathed by Aristotle. This point is worth lingering over, since in continental Europe it is widely believed that the metaphysical game was pretty much played out in Hegel, and there is a tendency to associate the new logic of Frege with the logical positivists, who welcomed it as a weapon to be used *against* metaphysics. The basic thought was attractive enough. Over the centuries philosophy has succeeded in establishing itself as a proper science in only one area—logic. Why not, then, junk the rest and confine philosophy henceforth to the logic of the empirical sciences?

Executing such a program was to prove by no means simple. In particular, it meant reckoning with the mathematical science of set theory, from which the new logic was felt to be virtually indistinguishable; thus the sentence 'Socrates is snub-nosed' came to be glossed by the logician as saying in effect that Socrates is a member of the set of snub-nosed people. Accordingly, the set of snub-nosed people emerges as the mathematical surrogate of Plato's snub-nosedness. Though it was natural enough to suppose that Plato's gropings in antiquity had at last been placed on a secure, scientific footing, such an estimate of the situation came to be recognized as at best premature, if only because of the gropings of mathematicians themselves, until they finally achieved (no thanks to the philosophers) their own so-called ZF intuition into the innermost nature of sets. It is, in fact, the innermost nature of everything which the metaphysician aims to address: witness Chapter 17, where sets in particular come to be understood in a much deeper fashion than mathematics alone can afford, and also Chapter 19, where current research into artificial intelligence positively invites the metaphysician to shatter traditional stereotypes regarding the link between the mental and the physical.

This emphasis on recent developments must not be allowed to obscure my commitment in the present volume to a quintessentially traditional approach, towards both philosophy in general and metaphysics in particular. *What* traditional metaphysics might be supposed to consist in, I am not prepared to accept at second hand. Thus, when Frege, in the course of arguing that a predicate like '*x* is snub-nosed' stands for a function in the mathematician's sense of the term, insists that functions are 'founded deep in the nature of things' (see Chapter 9), one knows that one is in the presence of metaphysics pure and simple. Metaphysics can even be defined, in sharp distinction to physics, with which it might otherwise be confused, as the theory of what lies founded deep in the nature of things. Classical metaphysics has thus been given a new lease of life, albeit in the most clandestine fashion, in the work of Frege. That Frege himself could only be astounded by the suggestion that he was a metaphysician merely indicates how very much closer to Aristotle we are today, thanks in no small measure to the Fregean revolution in logic. Inevitably, it was Kant who presided over all nineteenth-century attitudinizing in regard to metaphysics, and it can only be supposed that the protracted failure of philosophers to recognize the metaphysician in Frege attests to grave deficiencies in our proximate, Kantian heritage.

My own traditionalism is nowhere so evident as in my sustained effort to accommodate Kant, quite as much as Aristotle, within these pages, even while availing myself of all the advantages of hindsight afforded by the Fregean turn in philosophy, the clarification of which remained for W. V. Quine to effect in our own day by showing us how set theory—now recognized to be positively awash in Platonistic metaphysics—can and should be prevented from infecting logic proper. It is with just such a purified logic that I conjure in Chapters 4, 5, and 6, culminating in Quine's droll maxim, 'To be is to be the value of a variable.'[1] What Quine asks us to do in quasi-algebraic fashion is to 'solve' for x in the predicate 'x is snub-nosed', Socrates being one of the values of x. Quine's drollery was evident enough in the implicit conflation of such moribund Aristotelian jargon as 'being *qua* being' and the logico-mathematical idiom regarding the variables x, y, and z. Simply on the level of language, this refreshing interplay of old and new provided a first indication that philosophy was entering a new era, the age of Quine.

[1] See his 1948 paper 'On What There Is', in the *Review of Metaphysics*, reprinted in Quine, *From A Logical Point of View* (Cambridge, Mass.: Harvard University Press, 1961).

Part I

1

Qua

Scholars aside, few philosophers today are prepared to say that they have anything like a very clear notion of what Aristotle had in mind when he envisioned a theory of being *qua* being. That what he had in mind may be assumed to be decisive for metaphysics, now as well as then, they will readily concede; but, as in the natural sciences, questions of historical scholarship are felt to lie outside the discipline proper. With that position Aristotle would have heartily agreed, given that he sharply distinguished systematic from historical considerations. If historical considerations loom large in his *Metaphysics*, that merely attests to his having been self-consciously engaged in digesting and extending the work of his predecessors into an authoritative form that would render otiose any further consideration of either them or him, at any rate once he had succeeded in launching the new discipline.

Of the two words that enter into the formula 'being *qua* being', the easy one to elucidate is '*qua*', a gratuitous bit of Latin riding on the pristine Greek, *on heî on*, that translates simply into 'being as being', and that in the seventeenth century gave rise to the term 'ontology'. Although Kant salutes in passing 'the proud name of Ontology', he characteristically understands metaphysics to comprise the three sub-disciplines of rational (as contrasted with empirical) psychology, rational (as contrasted with physical) cosmology, and rational (as contrasted with revealed) theology, featuring respectively the soul, the world, and God. In taking ontology to be the core of metaphysics, I recognize an obligation to show precisely how soul, world, and God emerge thematically as ontological issues. A clue to understanding the role of *qua* in Aristotle's formula is provided by Dieter Henrich when he characterizes it as 'the particle of representation'. Metaphysics or ontology is presumably to be understood as the theory of something or other (waiving for the nonce what that might be) in so far as it is represented in a certain sort of way (as opposed to others).

What sort of way? Important in its own right, Quine's paradox of the mathematical bicyclist can be pressed into service here, affording us an indirect mode of access to the question.

Mathematicians may conceivably be said to be necessarily rational and not necessarily two-legged; and cyclists necessarily two-legged and not necessarily rational. But what of an individual who counts among his eccentricities both mathematics and cycling? Is this concrete individual necessarily rational and contingently two-legged or vice versa?[1]

In fact a formal contradiction can readily be derived when we consider the mathematical bicyclist Jones. If every bicyclist is necessarily two-legged, Jones is necessarily two-legged. But if no mathematician is necessarily two-legged, Jones is not necessarily two-legged. So Jones is both necessarily two-legged and not necessarily two-legged.

Quine's resolution of the paradox goes pretty much as follows. Jones is at once necessarily two-legged *qua* bicyclist and not necessarily two-legged *qua* mathematician. There is no inconsistency. It is like asking whether Chou is tall, when one is prepared to allow that he is tall for a Chinese, but not tall for an American. We may say that the predicate '*x* is tall' when taken out of context fails to express a property, while in context it is always to be taken as elliptical for '*x* is tall for an *F*' where the context determines how the *F* slot is to be filled. In the same way, Quine insists on taking the predicate '*x* is necessarily *F*' as elliptical for '*x* is necessarily *F qua* being a *G*'.

Now that the Latinism *qua* has been seen to pay its way as a technical device, we must take up two further pieces of Aristotelian jargon. An *essential* property of a thing is a property that not only belongs to it, but belongs to it necessarily, inextricably. The thing could not possibly exist in the absence of it. All other properties of a thing, being merely optional, are said to be *accidental* properties of that thing. According to Aristotle, there are

---

[1] W. V. Quine, *Word and Object* (Cambridge, Mass.: MIT Press, 1960), p. 199.

certain properties or attributes that Jones has essentially, others that he has accidentally (or contingently), and not merely *qua* bicyclist or *qua* mathematician but . . . how shall we put it? . . . *qua* Jones. There is a bit of a puzzle here. To consider Jones *qua* F or *qua* G is to represent Jones under a certain aspect, what Frege calls a 'mode of presentation'. To consider Jones *qua* Jones is presumably to represent him under the aspect of being himself, and one may well protest that there is no such *aspect*. One wants to say that considering Jones *qua* Jones—if only such an enterprise were feasible—would consist in considering 'this concrete individual' not under this or that aspect, but purely referentially, in terms of himself. But we also want to say that to consider Jones *qua* anything (for that is what *qua* is all about) *is* to represent him in a certain way, under a certain aspect. Is Aristotle, then, engaged in playing an incoherent, double game when he undertakes (in particular) to consider Socrates *qua* Socrates—Socrates and his snub-nosedness are favourite examples of his, the one going proxy for any entity, the other for any accidental property—and (more generally) being *qua* being? For metaphysics is designed by Aristotle to be precisely the general theory of what (essentially) each and everything is *qua* itself.

In the case of any particular F one should have no difficulty in understanding what it is to consider the F as an F—for example, the dance as a dance. Witness the following disreputable piece of doggerel:

> There once was a girl from Australia
> Who went to a dance as a dahlia.
> At the start of the ball
> Her petals did fall,
> So the dance as a dance was a failure.

Although metaphysical jargon regarding being *qua* being proves to be by no means as far removed from the vernacular as one might suppose, it is one thing to consider the bicyclist as a bicyclist (or even as a mathematician) and quite another to consider Jones as Jones. How is the latter to be done? Aristotle's answer is simple: by recognizing Jones's essential properties.

2

Relativism

How can one tell, protests the anti-essentialist, simply on the basis of observation, which of Jones's manifest properties are so inextricably linked to his very *being*—that is, his existence—that they can even be said by Aristotle to constitute it? That this or that property belongs or fails to belong to Jones, observation can establish readily enough; but how can mere sense perception reveal the presence of an unbreakable link that ties Jones to this and not to that property? Well, there is always the rational faculty to consult. But this faculty can assure us at best, persists the anti-essentialist, only that being two-legged, say, is essential to being a bicyclist, not that it is essential to being 'this concrete individual' who happens to be a bicyclist. One can at least argue that two-leggedness is built into the very concept of what is involved in being a bicyclist, though even here there is doubtless plenty of room for quibbling. Might not one of our new breed of resourceful amputees surprise us by 'pedalling' a bicycle upside down using only his hands? No matter. The point of Quine's somewhat frivolous example is clear. A necessary connection between a thing and a property is far more problematic than one between concepts.

By insisting that it is only relative to his being a bicyclist that Jones can be allowed to be essentially—that is, necessarily—two-legged, an anti-essentialist like Quine may be said to be a relativist when it comes to essence and accident. That Jones is essentially rational one is free to assert, but only as long as one adds, let it be only in a whisper, '*qua* mathematician', or even '*qua* human being'. The idiom of essence and accident is simply too useful, outside as well as within philosophy, to be readily dispensed with; one has merely to cease employing it in the naïve, absolutist mode to which, the anti-essentialist ruefully confesses, we are all too naturally prone, in order to discover this. One example may suffice. How can it be doubted that every human being, and *a fortiori* Jones in particular, is essentially a human being, absolutely speaking? I raise the question here merely to indicate the difference between essentialist and anti-essentialist. The latter will acquiesce in the essence/accident idiom only if it is at least tacitly relativized to context. The former does not reject the relativized mode, for he, too, feels free to have recourse to it whenever convenient; but the essentialist also insists on employing the language of essence and accident in the absolute mode, as when he says *sans phrase* that Jones is essentially a human being. Or, if you will, that Jones is essentially a human being *qua* Jones.

Because someone like Quine is a relativist when it comes to essence and accident, it must not be assumed that he is a relativist as such, in his ontology, which he is not. Every philosopher is a relativist about something or other, for the relativizing trick is simply too attractive to be left to the relativist as his exclusive possession. What it might be like to be a relativist proper—that is to say, a metaphysical relativist—is nowhere so succinctly expressed as in the following fragments from Plato's *Theaetetus*, at 152b and 157a, where Socrates undertakes to play the devil's advocate on behalf of Protagoras.

Is it not true that sometimes, when the same wind blows, one of us feels cold, and the other does not?
Certainly.
Then in that case, shall we say that the wind is in itself cold or not cold; or shall we accept Protagoras' saying that it is cold for him who feels cold and not cold for him who does not?
Apparently.
And all the rest—hard and hot and so forth—must be regarded in the same way: we must assume . . . that nothing exists in itself.

Although the wind *is* cold relative to my perception of it, it is not cold relative to yours. Accordingly, in itself, absolutely speaking, the wind is neither cold nor not cold. And what holds good here for coldness can be seen to apply equally to any other property of the wind. Furthermore, the wind itself is merely an example, and we are thus invited to generalize from it to the conclusion that neither the wind nor anything else can be said to exist in itself, absolutely speaking, but only relative to other things. Especially to be noticed in the Platonic text is the informal use twice over of the expression 'in itself', or *kath' hauto* (literally, 'according to itself'), which is subsequently enshrined as a technical or quasi-technical term in Aristotle's expanded definition of metaphysics as the theory of being *qua* being and the attributes that belong to this *kath' hauto*, or 'in virtue of its own nature', in the Oxford translation of *Metaphysics*, 4. 1. 1003a20. Having recourse now to two pieces of Latinate jargon, we can say that for Aristotle metaphysics is the general theory of (*a*) what each and every thing is essentially *qua* itself and (*b*) the attributes that belong to the thing *per se*.

If (*a*) draws on the distinction between essential and accidental properties, why not view (*b*) in the light of the *Theaetetus* passage, thereby taking it to draw on the very different distinction between those properties that belong to a thing absolutely speaking, as opposed to those that belong to it only relative to something else? In rejecting Protagorean relativism, Aristotle must insist that while some properties of a thing are merely relational (for example, being a sister), others are non-relational or absolute in character, belonging to it by virtue of itself—that is, *kath' hauto*, or *per se*. Of these *per se* attributes, so understood, some will be merely accidental, others essential, the latter emerging in their turn as *per se* attributes of the thing in an emphatically strong sense of the term, by contrast with non-relational but accidental properties (for example, the whiteness of Socrates), which are no longer felt to belong to it by virtue of its *very* self—that is, its being. Metaphysics undertakes, then, to investigate what appertains to each and every thing *per se*, both in the strong and in the weak sense of the term, the one primarily where *per se* contrasts with *per accidens*, the other in a secondary fashion where *per se* contrasts with *per aliud*.

If the foregoing characterization fits Aristotelian metaphysics well enough, it hardly seems acceptable as an account of metaphysics as such if Protagorean relativism is to be accommodated under its umbrella, since the latter takes every property of a thing to be of the *per aliud* variety. More important still as a counter-example is relativism as such, of which the perceptual relativism of Protagoras is merely one variety. Looking ahead to recent developments, there is a conceptual variety of relativism that can only be understood as a specifically modern phenomenon, whose very intelligibility presupposes the great impact of Kant. According to this post-Kantian conceptual relativism, although mountains (to choose an arbitrary example) exist plainly enough relative to our standard, common-sense conceptual scheme, there are other, equally valid conceptualizations of the world wherein mountains simply do not exist at all, or at least wherein mountains as such are conspicuously absent from the furniture of the world. In fact, on this view, nothing exists in itself, absolutely speaking, but only relative to this or that conceptual scheme, while at the same time the thing fails to exist relative to others. Conceptual relativism goes by the somewhat fashionable name today of anti-realism, and one can readily understand why it is said to offer us (in Michael Dummett's words) a 'picture of reality as an amorphous lump not yet articulated into discrete objects'.

'But what would it be like to omit mountains from a valid conceptualization of the world?', someone might ask in bewilderment. Well, consider a radical form of eliminative materialism that acknowledges only the ultimate particles of physics —quarks, let us say—and absolutely nothing else. In particular —and this is Peter van Inwagen's query[1]—why suppose that *these* particles packed fairly closely together constitute a macro-entity, namely Mount Everest, whereas *those*, of equal number, scattered pretty much at random throughout the universe, fail to add up to anything beyond their very own selves? In the name of a 'budget' ontology, Occam's razor alone, with its demand for parsimony, should suffice to eliminate all macro-entities across the board, while 'a taste for desert landscapes' (purloining a trope of Quine's) might be expected to render the prospect especially attractive.

[1] See his forthcoming *Material Beings* (Ithaca: Cornell University Press, 1988).

3

Dialectical Devices

If metaphysics in the narrow sense of the word is to be identified with ontology, no purer metaphysical doctrine can possibly be found than the Protagorean thesis that to be (anything at all) is to be relative (to something or other). Tightening the screw a bit further, we might add that for the Protagorean, to be as such *is* to be relative, thereby helping ourselves thematically to one more dialectical turn of speech, namely 'as such'. Less obviously perhaps, particularly considering the difficulty we encountered in stretching Aristotle's definition of ontology so that it might accommodate Protagoras, the latter will even be seen to be committed to a doctrine of being *qua* being. One would antecedently expect as much, given that Aristotle's definition of ontology (he never uses the word 'metaphysics', choosing to label his undertaking as 'first philosophy') is designed to encompass doctrines very much opposed to his own. At the end of Chapter 1, however, it was not only Protagoras, but even an anti-relativist like Quine who appeared to be ruled out of court, as an anti-essentialist.

How precisely metaphysics, or ontology, is to be defined is not a question that greatly interests the contemporary philosopher, probably owing to a surfeit of methodological discussion during the heyday of the logical positivists and Wittgenstein, when no substantive issue of metaphysics loomed as large as the methodological question regarding the cognitive standing of the enterprise as such. Although that question engages Aristotle's attention to no small degree, when we come to Kant it takes over entirely. What Kant means by his 'critique of pure reason' proves to be nothing but an examination of rationality in its metaphysical employment. But, while I share the impatience of contemporary philosophers regarding any further protracted involvement in the methodology of metaphysics (Kant and Wittgenstein being felt to be quite enough), my historical sense

warns me that the pendulum may well have swung too far in the
opposite direction. Because the philosopher as such is concerned
with the eternal, even today historical considerations remain very
foreign to him; and the kind of 'mix' of the one with the other
which saturates these pages tends to leave him feeling distinctly
uneasy. How the historical sense might actually serve the philosopher, albeit in a subordinate capacity, as an 'early warning
system' may already be evidenced by the case at hand.

Challenged almost from the outset by the two very demanding,
substantive issues of essentialism and relativism, we are not likely
to be blown off course by the gales of methodology. One might
wish, however, to be somewhat clearer as to how relativism and
anti-essentialism qualify as ontological doctrines. Relativism is
the harder case to handle. Although Chapter 1 left the impression
that the doctrine of essence is the (true) theory of being *qua* being,
Chapter 2 showed that the anti-essentialist can be accommodated
by Aristotle's expanded definition of ontology, which extends to
any property of a thing that belongs to it *per se*, where that can be
taken to apply to any of its non-relational features, as in the
Theaetetus. Even this liberalized version of ontology fails, however, to secure a niche for the relativist.

The easy solution is simply to decree that the relativist has a
(negative) theory of both essential and absolute being: namely,
that nothing has any *per se* attributes in either the strong sense
of *per se*, meaning essential, or the weak sense, signifying non-
relational or absolute. Although such a decree need not be
disreputably *ad hoc*, by accentuating the negative it fails to
honour our present finding that when it is insisted that to be as
such is to be relative, an eminently pure thesis of ontology is
being advanced. While marginal, and even deviant, ontologies or
quasi-ontologies will doubtless have to be recognized somewhere
along the line, relativism, precisely because it projects a
paradigmatic theory of being *qua* being, cannot be relegated to
the periphery of the discipline. We turn now to a proof that *any*
doctrine of being as such is a doctrine of being *qua* being. I use the
word 'proof' advisedly, for it is the very logic of these dialectical
devices—'as such' and *qua*—that is involved, and the word
'logic' itself is being scrupulously respected, given that logical

entailment is featured. The proof proceeds by way of generalization from a single case. Imagine a book entitled *The Econom-
ics of War* that begins, 'By no means a study of war as such, the
present work focuses on war solely as an economic phenomenon.
In the final volume in this series (the series is entitled *War*) General McArthur will address war *as* war.' A study of war as such
being seen to be inevitably a study of war as war and vice versa,
the logical equivalence that obtains here between the two items
cannot be merely a local affair, but must apply across the board
to discourse concerning anything whatever, and Protagoras in
particular must thus be credited with having a doctrine of being
qua being. Contrasting the locutions 'war as war' and 'being as
being', it is the former that 'wears the trousers' in the sense that,
whenever we fear that we may be losing control over our metaphysical jargon, we must refresh our intuitions by examining how
these dialectical devices are used outside philosophy. Such lack of
control is instanced by the very fact of entertaining a doubt as
to whether, in the absence of a theory of being *qua* being, the
relativist might not yet have a theory of being as such. How
these dialectical devices function in all sorts of discourse, outside
as well as inside philosophy, Aristotle expressly calls upon the
metaphysician to investigate, and we have seen how a bit of doggerel can provide him with data no less relevant than scholarly
discourse on war. As between a study of war as an economic
phenomenon and a study of war as war, the latter must be
allowed at least to smack of ontology, and at a pinch one might
even venture to speak of the ontology of war.

That the study of the dialectical devices as they function outside philosophy can contribute to ontology as such has already
been shown. Thanks to being recognized, finally, as a theory of
being *qua* being, relativism must be accepted as falling within
Aristotle's definition of ontology. Indeed it is essentialism (and
anti-essentialism) that needs to be reassigned. In its concern with
both being *qua* being and the attributes that belong to a thing *per
se*, ontology has a secondary, as well as a primary, mission. First
and foremost, it seeks to determine, in its theory of what it is to be
as such, whether relativism is true, in either its classical,
Protagorean form or its modern, post-Kantian version. Only if

relativism turns out to be false can ontology embark on its secondary mission. For it is only after we are satisfied that things exist in themselves, absolutely speaking, that the quarrel between essentialists and anti-essentialists acquires any bite; only then can we investigate whether the *per se* attributes of a thing are merely to be identified with its non-relational features. Concerned primarily with a (positive or negative) doctrine of the absolute, the metaphysician, on the present account, proves to be involved only secondarily in a (positive or negative) doctrine of essence.

The order of priorities has been strikingly reversed. In the previous chapter the metaphysician was seen to be principally concerned with a doctrine of essence and only secondarily (albeit preliminarily) engaged in establishing that there are indeed non-relational properties. Although Aristotle may be entitled to his scheme, he is hardly being methodologically neutral when it comes to the substantive issues of relativism and essentialism. Aristotle's scheme may well be the right one taken *in itself*. Even so, more suitable *to us*—the idiom here is pure Aristotle—is the present, reversed version of it. In the same vein it can be said that if 'war as war', relative to us, with our limitations, is to be accorded (cognitional) priority over 'being as being', it is rather 'being as being' that takes (logical) precedence over 'war as war', for the latter is only a special case of the former. Welcome additions to our portfolio of dialectical devices, 'to us' and 'in itself' can even help to elucidate Aristotle's own characterization of his enterprise, not as metaphysics or even ontology, but as first— that is, primary—philosophy, addressed to what is fundamental or primary in itself. If the physicist supposes that the fundamental question concerns the precise nature of the ultimate constituents of which everything else is composed, he is mistaken. More fundamental still is the question of whether Protagoras is right in his conviction that nothing exists in itself, absolutely speaking, but only relative to other things; for it is here that the 'in itself' comes to sight as such.

4

Herr Krug's Pen

As the prototypical relativist, Protagoras finds his opposite number across the centuries in Hegel, for it is with Hegel above all that one inevitably associates the absolute, certainly the absolute as such. But if Protagoras is the easiest of philosophers to understand, Hegel is the most difficult, and in the English-speaking world at least, the professional philosopher even tends to pride himself on *not* being able to understand him. Accordingly, one can only be grateful to the immortal Herr Krug for providing us with an anecdotal point of entry into his thought. When Herr Krug challenged Hegel to deduce his pen from the absolute, the philosopher contented himself with the reply that he had more important things to do. The episode is instructive, positively inviting one to recall Schopenhauer's sneering characterization of Hegel's system as 'a monstrous amplification of the Ontological Argument'. Although it is scarcely credible that Hegel supposed himself to be in possession of an 'ontological argument' for such trivialities as Herr Krug's pen, he declined to convict Herr Krug of any outright misunderstanding of his position.

Waiving the merits of the Ontological Argument, it has been standardly assumed that the existence of something can never be established by pure logic alone. Non-existence, of course, is different. One proves that there are no F's—for example, round squares—by using logic to derive a contradiction from the concept of F-ness; and it is precisely here, in such proofs, that we find the clearest examples of a priori (as contrasted with a posteriori) knowledge—that is, knowledge that is not based on any premises supplied by experience. Hegel aside, this standard view of logic has been in effect rejected by two philosophers above all: Anselm in the eleventh century, with his Ontological Argument for the existence of God (see Chapter 11 below), and Frege in the nineteenth, with *his* ontological argument—no other character-ization will do—for the existence of numbers. One of the best-kept secrets of our time, Frege's role in this connection can scarcely be exaggerated. Purely by means of logic (a logic, indeed, expressly designed for that purpose), Frege undertakes to prove in a priori fashion not merely that there are no round squares, but that there *are* numbers, which exist outside space and time independently of mind (see Chapter 14 below). Styled 'abstract entities' by Quine, such items inevitably recall Plato's Forms, thanks in particular to the fact some of those in Plato's immediate entourage even ventured to identify the Forms with numbers. As anti-Platonists, most philosophers have followed Aristotle in his insistence that to be as such is to be concrete, as opposed to abstract, where even God is a concrete entity.

In addition to abstract entities in general and numbers in par-ticular, God emerges readily enough as a specific theme of ontology. Relying on the standard view of logic, Hume insists that one can deny the existence of anything whatever, free of the fear that logic might convict one of an inconsistency. To be, then, for Hume is to be contingent (as opposed to necessary), and the Ontological Argument of Anselm thus provides an intriguing counter-example to Hume's thesis. For the argument undertakes to establish that just as the statement 'There is at least one round square' harbours an inconsistency, so, too, a deep enough under-standing of the very concept of God allows one to derive by logic a contradiction from the statement 'There is no God' or 'God fails to exist'. The statement being thus shown to be not merely false, but necessarily false as a point of logic, God is correspond-ingly found not merely to exist, but to exist in defiance of Hume as a non-contingent entity; and Anselm is found to be urging in effect that the statement 'God exists' expresses an analytic (as opposed to a synthetic) proposition, defined as a proposition whose truth can be established solely by logic. In the same vein, 'There are numbers' comes to be certified as analytic in the new logic of Frege. The whole issue regarding what can and what cannot be proved by logic alone now emerges as absolutely crit-ical for metaphysics, thereby raising the prior issue of what exactly logic is supposed to be anyway.

That metaphysics bears a special affinity to logic, no one has trumpeted as loudly as Hegel, when he entrusted his metaphysics to a work entitled *The Science of Logic*. Although there is almost nothing in the work that is recognizable as logic proper, Hegel wishes to argue that rationality as such—one recalls Kant's 'pure reason'—is to be found in logic above all. Moreover, he does not hesitate to concede that logic proper involves an abstraction of form from content. When it comes to determining whether some argument featuring 'All men are mortal' as one of its premisses is valid, it is only the logical form of the premiss, *sans* content— namely, 'Every *F* is a *G*'—that the logician need consider. It is at this point that Hegel makes his radical move, arguing that a purely internal critique of formal logic as such cannot but smash the barrier between form and content, thereby inviting the full content of the world to come flooding in. In one way or another, then, the rational reconstruction of formal logic (= metaphysics) is found to provide a deduction of Herr Krug's pen, though it may be supposed that what we now take logical deduction to be will itself undergo a radical transformation. Far from having a purely aprioristic character, as Schopenhauer supposed, the deduction will presumably proceed by way of a breakdown of the barrier separating a priori from a posteriori. Having languished in a decadent state in Hegel's time, formal logic took its one great leap beyond Aristotle in 1879, with the publication of Frege's *Begriffsschrift*. There, indeed, as if by magic, one finds all the machinery necessary to execute a crisp deduction of Herr Krug's pen simply from the Principle of Identity.

If only as a technical exercise, the metaphysician cannot refrain from examining the deduction at close quarters. There are in fact two mini-arguments, one building on the other. First, one argues as follows. Everything is identical with itself, therefore Smith is identical with Smith (the name 'Smith' having been assigned to Herr Krug's pen). The second argument proceeds thus. Smith is identical with Smith, therefore something is identical with Smith. Enshrined in our standard notation, the two-stage argument may be displayed as follows.

(1) (x) $x = x$

∴ (2) Smith = Smith U.I.

∴ (3) $(\exists x)$ $(x = $ Smith) E.G.

Taking (1) to read, 'For every x, x is identical with x', we deduce (2) from it by appealing to the Rule of Universal Instantiation, and from (2) we deduce in its turn (3), which reads, 'There exists an x such that x is identical with Smith'. Here we invoke the Rule of Existential Generalization. If this 'deduction' of Herr Krug's pen from the Principle of Identity should be thought to have an Alice-in-Wonderland quality about it, fair enough. The 'Alice' books do in fact provide the poetic counterpart of metaphysics, and it is no accident that they are especially treasured by logicians.

Why a logician might take the argument to be valid by virtue of its form is seen readily enough by taking a simple case: for example, 'Everything is a man; therefore Moscow is a man,' where the logical form is seen to be 'Everything is an F; therefore a is an F,' the point of course being that if, absurdly enough, everything is supposed to be a man, then the city of Moscow can hardly fail to be one as well. The next step is to ensure that our universal premiss can be known to be true on a priori grounds.

Seeing that everything is either a man or it is not a man (by the so-called Law of the Excluded Middle), it follows that Smith is either a man or he is not a man, and in either case, according to standard logic today (there are always non-standard, deviant systems on the market), Smith's existence is assured. Should one feel that the proper name 'Smith' stands in the way of what we really want—namely, a proof of Herr Krug's pen both as a pen and as his—I believe that, thanks to his extended notion of a proper name, Frege allows the following argument to be formally valid. Everything is identical with itself; therefore Herr Krug's pen is identical with itself; therefore something is identical with Herr Krug's pen.

If the philosopher instinctively recoils from Frege's deduction it is in part because of the widespread conviction that the conclusion of any formally valid argument ought to be somehow 'contained' in its premisses. It is felt that the conclusion of any valid argument ought to be deducible from its premisses on a purely a priori basis. Call this 'the aprioristic thesis', which Frege's deduction conspicuously violates. There is thus a striking difference between Frege's aprioristic proof of numbers and his aposterioristic proof of Herr Krug's pen; for it is only the former that can properly be classified (with a salute to Anselm) as an ontological argument for the existence of something. Someone who has never heard of Herr Krug or his pen would hardly be able to deduce the existence of Herr Krug's pen simply from the Principle of Identity. Frege is thus seen to be fulfilling the Hegelian imperative, as logical form and empirical content cease to be severed from one another. Regarding 'the aim of my concept-script', Frege wrote in 1880 or 1881, 'right from the start I had in mind *the expression of a content* . . ., not a *calculus* restricted to pure logic' (emphasis original).

It turns out now that, although almost no philosopher today can rest easy with Frege's aposterioristic deduction of Herr Krug's pen, virtually all are prepared to reject the aprioristic thesis once they have been given the opportunity to ponder the following argument, namely '(4), (5), therefore (3)'.

(4) It is raining.
(5) It is not raining.

Confessedly bizarre, the argument has the simple form 'p, ~ p ∴ q' which at least since medieval times has been recognized by logicians as a valid form of argument. Thus, from (4) one is entitled to derive '(4) x (3)' by the Rule of Addition, otherwise styled the Rule of Dilution. And from '(4) x (3)' taken along with (5) one derives (3) by the Rule of Disjunctive Syllogism. If there are indeed a few philosophers today who, preferring the non-standard, so-called 'relevance' logic of Alan Ross Anderson and Nuel Belnap, spurn the argument on the ground that the Rule of Addition is not to be credited as a properly valid principle of inference, one suspects that they are motivated largely by their allegiance to the aprioristic thesis. For how could someone who has never heard of Herr Krug or his pen succeed in deducing '(4) x (3)' simply from (4)?

5

Truth

Metaphysics aside, one would have thought that hard-core logic was one thing on which one could fully rely, and that a specifically logical approach to metaphysics (were that but possible) would thus offer the prospect of reducing the subject to a proper science. If the previous chapter cannot fail to have a sobering effect in that regard, one reliable principle does appear to have emerged: namely, the Principle of Identity, which allows us to insist that to be as such is to be self-identical, where confirmation of the point is at hand in the readiness with which we are urged today to write '$(\exists x)\, x = x$' in order to say that there is something, not nothing, as if being self-identical were scarcely to be distinguished from just being—that is, existing. More than that, we can argue that the property of being self-identical is one that even Protagoras's wind has in itself, absolutely speaking, apart from its relations to other things. And as if that were not enough, why not press our advantage by insisting that this property of the wind can be conceived to be only an essential, not an accidental, feature of it, not merely *qua* some *F* or some *G*, but *qua* the very thing itself? Being self-identical is thus seen to be the metaphysical property par excellence, affording us access at once to essence and the absolute.

Accorded the logico-ontological status of an absolute, the Principle of Identity can be snappily expressed by the slogan 'No entity without *self*-identity'. Logico-ontological? Is that not precisely the kind of pretentious jargon that infects metaphysics at its worst? Well, yes, it *is* of that general kind, but I propose to show in detail how the present occasion is an exception, exempt from all reproach. Moreover, the case at hand is important enough to serve as an object lesson in metaphysics good and bad. The issue comes down to this: why not simply admit the Principle of Identity as a truth of logic and have done with it? One recalls how Kant rebuked the dogmatic metaphysicians of his day for padding their treaties with analytic statements and their tedious demonstrations, as if such statements could be expected to play any but a very subordinate role when it comes to a discussion of substantive issues. In fact, *the* metaphysical fallacy according to Kant, of which he convicted the entire tradition, consists precisely in the error of supposing that mere logic can suffice on its own to produce substantive conclusions when, as a purely formal discipline that abstracts from content, it is equipped to play only an ancillary role in the cognitive enterprise. Nowhere is that fallacy more manifest than in Anselm's Ontological Argument which Kant is thus committed to refuting. Along the same lines, our own logical approach to metaphysics might well be felt to be still more objectionable, a vicious anachronism. A typical analytic proposition like 'All bodies are extended' serves merely to analyze the content of a concept—in the present case, the concept 'body', which, on being unpacked, can be seen to be equivalent to that of a substance extended in three dimensions. Already contained in the concept 'body', the word 'extended' in our statement merely renders explicit what has already been thought by us implictly from the outset. Negation of the statement would thus amount to saying: 'Some substances extended in three dimensions are not extended.' So it is scarcely surprising that logic can be used to prove it. Closer to home, 'self-identical' as it figures in the statement 'Every wind is self-identical' likewise fails to add anything substantive to the content of 'wind'. In sharp contrast, synthetic propositions like 'All swans are white' involve the bringing together of two logically independent concepts, in this case 'swan' and 'white', for no contradiction can be derived from 'Some swans are not white', black swans having in fact been discovered in Australia. Accordingly, we must turn to synthetic propositions if we want to extend our knowledge beyond what is contained in our concepts.

In an autobiographical vein, I recall my keen disappointment years ago on first reading Aristotle's *Metaphysics*, precisely at the point where, having defined his undertaking, technically, as the theory of being *qua* being, Aristotle proceeds at great length to defend the Principle of Non-contradiction against a whole range of what I could only regard as more or less specious objections, insisting that the principle expresses the fundamental truth regarding being as such. One understood Aristotle's point, of course. That no attribute can both belong and yet fail to belong to a thing, at any rate at one and the same time, might well be taken in some devious fashion to constitute an essential feature of anything whatever, and though one understood the principle in the first instance as a truth of logic proper (no inconsistent proposition is true), one was prepared to allow that it could be construed in the material—that is, ontological—as well as in the formal—that is, logical—mode. Being analytic, however, in either mode, the principle, even while it could be said to have a logico-ontological status, must surely be denied the pride of place in metaphysics that Aristotle chose to accord it. Here I felt Kant had to be right. If auxiliary principles of metaphysics might be analytic, primary ones would have to be synthetic. One could not expect to show that their denial involved a formal inconsistency of logic. Because those sentiments remain widely, if not quite universally, shared today, it is incumbent on me to explain how I can now propose to accord to the Principle of Identity, itself an analytic proposition, the pride of place that was assigned by Aristotle to the Principle of Non-contradiction. First, a methodological point: nothing can count as a basic principle of metaphysics that fails to excite serious controversy. Otherwise metaphysics will be trivially vindicated as a viable undertaking quite apart from any effort to allay the misgivings of Hume, Kant, and Wittgenstein. Any such redefinition of the term—for that is what it would amount to—could only be an insult to the memory of those philosophical watch-dogs whom the metaphysician must never cease to cherish for providing him with an 'early warning system' against some of the fatuities to which he is only too liable to succumb.

But where is serious controversy over the Principle of Identity to be found? Does anyone suppose that there could be a thing somewhere that might fail to be identical with itself? Put baldly like that, the answer, of course, is no. How, then, do we explain the difficulty? A historical remark may provide a point of entry. According to Wittgenstein, when the philosopher says 'Everything is identical with itself', he is merely mouthing words which, by being concatenated as they are, have been deprived of all meaning.[1] I mention the point only to move on. Wittgenstein's position strikes the contemporary philosopher as so tendentiously perverse, at any rate in its raw form, that he can only brush it aside with impatience. Let me adopt a more ingratiating approach. A close study of such refractory topics as the Liar Paradox has brought some of our ablest philosophers to the reluctant conclusion that language and thought can function only within the constraints of a 'universe of discourse' that must of necessity fall short of encompassing the universe as such. On any occasion of utterance, then, the Principle of Identity must be taken as an elliptical way of saying that everything within some restricted domain of entities is self-identical. Why the Liar Paradox in particular is often felt to coerce one in that manner can be understood most vividly after it is seen to constitute a *logical* paradox in the precise sense of the term, contrary to a widespread view (associated with the name of Frank Ramsey) that takes it to express a 'merely' semantic—that is, linguistic—puzzle.

Remembered for his offhand remark 'All Cretans are liars', it is rather the following precise argument that Epimenides the Cretan advanced, the conclusion being stated exactly at midnight, the premiss a few seconds before: 'No utterance made by a Cretan at midnight is an utterance that succeeds in expressing a true proposition,' therefore, 'No utterance that succeeds in expressing a true proposition is an utterance made by a Cretan at midnight.' Exhibiting the logical form 'No *F* is a *G*. Therefore, no *G* is an *F*', the argument must be certified as formally valid, which means of course that if the first statement is true, the second must be true as well. Given that the second is an utterance made by a Cretan at midnight, it cannot be true (for if it were true, it would be false). Accordingly, the first statement cannot be true either. Suppose now (the simplest case) that the second statement is the only utterance ever made by a Cretan at midnight. Then the first will be true after all, and a formally valid argument with a single, true premiss will terminate in a conclusion that fails to be true. Although the second statement

[1] Ludwig Wittgenstein, *Philosophical Investigations* (Blackwell, Oxford: 1953), Part I, Sections 215–16, pp. 84–5.

taken on its own might seem to be sufficiently paradoxical in the absence of the first, one popular response has been to insist that, thanks to being suicidally self-referential, the second fails to express any proposition whatever, be it true or false. Anticipating that move, our new version of the puzzle undertakes to display a formally valid argument with a true premiss and a non-true conclusion, thereby confronting us with a contradiction in terms.

The response of the Tarski school to the Liar now proves to be more difficult to resist than before. In reply to Pilate's question 'What is truth?', the Tarskians pose a question of their own: 'Are you referring to $truth_0$ or to $truth_1$ or to $truth_2$, etc.?', on the ground that the Liar has succeeded in exposing a deep incoherence in the very notion of truth plain and simple. On the lowest (object = 0) level, sentences like 'No horses fly' and 'Some horses fly' are seen to be $true_0$ or $false_0$, though the words 'true' and 'false' are not allowed to appear in any object-level sentence. It is on level 1 that we find statements like 'The sentence "No horses fly" is true'; such statements, being meta-linguistic in character, are $true_1$ or $false_1$. On level 2 the sentences have a meta-meta-linguistic character: for example, 'The sentence I used to illustrate sentences on level 1 is true.' Such sentences will be $true_2$ or $false_2$. Systematically ambiguous, the word 'true' will express a different property on each level; thus, if someone says 'Every true sentence is true', his utterance must be pegged at some specific level—for example, 36. At best he can be understood only to be saying in effect something like 'Every true sentence with the possible exception of this one is true'; though that is much too optimistic an assessment, since all sentences on a level equal to or greater than 36 lie outside the domain of the utterance.

The Tarskian approach has far-reaching consequences. In providing a semantics for such logical jargon as '$p \times q$' we make use of the following truth table, thereby ruling that '$p \times q$' is true when either p or q is true, but is otherwise false.

p	q	$p \times q$
T	T	T
T	F	T
F	T	T
F	F	F

Unfortunately, truth as such is no longer recognized by the Tarskians. There is no explaining the conditions under which '$p \times q$' is just plain true. It, too, will be systematically ambiguous, depending on whether we are invoking $truth_0$ or $truth_1$ or $truth_2$ and so on. Finally, what are the truth conditions of the sentence '$(x) \; x = x$'? Here again we need to distinguish $truth_0$ conditions, $truth_1$ conditions, $truth_2$ conditions, and so forth. As long as we stick to everything on the object level—that is, nature *sans* mind—we are on safe ground. On this level, the Principle of Identity is of course $true_0$, but we are no longer making a statement about everything, and in fact any such statement is ruled out as incoherent in principle. Since logic itself is replaced by $logic_0$, $logic_1$, $logic_2$, and so on, where each operates on its own level, the very expression 'the Principle of Identity' ceases to refer to some one thing; having now a proxy on each level of discourse, 'it' (and here I am violating the Tarskian taboo) must be taken to assert on each level that everything to be found on the levels below it is self-identical.

Precise content can now be given to the otherwise pretentious thesis that the Principle of Identity expresses a fundamental truth of metaphysics. First and foremost, by insisting that the Principle enjoys unrestricted application, one is committed to a rejection of the whole Tarskian programme. We can now even say, oddly enough, that one research project assigned to metaphysics as such consists in providing an anti-Tarskian resolution of the Liar Paradox, couched in particular as a paradox of logic. Only after completing that task is the metaphysician entitled to insist that to be as such and not merely to be on this or that level is to be self-identical. Coming to sight successively as a puzzle of semantics, logic and metaphysics, the Liar can no longer be shunted off to the margins of philosophy as so many philosophers have been inclined to do, preferring to regard it as scarcely more than a piece of linguistic pathology. In particular, because metaphysics must be allowed to use the universal quantifier 'everything' to range over *everything* it has a vested interest in an anti-Tarskian solution to the Liar.

6

Ontological Commitment

Himself a relativist in regard to truth, Alfred Tarski allows a statement to be true—that is, true_0 or true_1 or true_2 and so on—only relative to some restricted universe of discourse, thereby ruling out the Protagorean doctrine, with its unabashed reference to everything, as semantically ill formed. One is thus tempted to say that whereas Tarski is anti-metaphysical root and branch, Protagoras is only speciously so. In fact, I hereby affirm just that, in the cool idiom of ontology. Committed to the doctrine that to be as such is always to be relative (whether to conception or perception, is a secondary issue), the metaphysical relativist will be allowed to have an ontology.

That the point is by no means routine, it suffices merely to mention Quine, with his famous 'criterion of ontological commitment'. No substantive principle of ontology in its own right, 'To be is to be the value of a variable' serves rather as a hermeneutic, whereby one may read off a philosopher's ontology from his informal discussions. How one applies Quine's criterion in a particular case, the following statements should help elucidate.

(1) All men are mortal.
(2) (x) x is a man $\supset$ x is a mortal.
(3) 5 is a man $\supset$ 5 is mortal.

Suppose that our philosopher subscribes to (1) in his theory of the world. Inviting his co-operation, we translate (1) into the 'canonical notation' of standard logic and urge him to accept (2) as well. In fact, (2) involves a subtle transformation of (1), since it is to be read as saying that for any x whatever—for example, Herr Krug's pen—if that x happens by chance to be a man, then it is mortal. Where (1) is Tarskian in spirit owing to its very restricted use of the universal quantifier 'all', (2) is defiantly anti-Tarskian by

'quantifying over' everything whatever. Here, then, is one critical point at which the science of logic, which one might reason-
ably suppose to be neutral when it comes to philosophy proper,
takes on a positively metaphysical character at the hands of Frege
and Quine. Digging in his heels for that very reason, our philosopher may refuse to be cajoled by us into the acceptance of (2),
and we shall then feel entitled to strike his name off the list of
ontologists. More important is the case where, having acquiesced
in (2), our philosopher is led on to consider (3). Does (3) 'follow'
from (2) by the Rule of Universal Instantiation? Well, that all
depends on whether 5 really exists. If it does, yes; if not, no. The
rules of the game (as standardly played) do not allow one to
accept (3) as true (on the ground perhaps that it is merely 'hypo-
thetical') if one is unsure of the 'ontological status' of 5—that is,
whether it exists or not. Only if our philosopher believes that
there exists an x such that it is identical with 5 does 5 prove to be
one of the *values* of the variable x as it features in (2) that he is
prepared to acknowledge in his ontology.

The example was not chosen fortuitously. The question as to
whether or not there are numbers, Quine takes as his paradigm of
an ontological question, and his criterion of ontological commitment as it applies across the board was expressly devised with
reference to that one case above all. One can even say that our
own post-Wittgensteinian era was launched precisely by the following argument of Quine. (1) It is physics that constitutes (the
core of) the true theory of the world. But (2) physics requires
mathematics. And (3) mathematics requires numbers (or sets).
Therefore, (4) there are numbers (or sets). But note the radical
difference between Quine's argument for numbers and Frege's.
Purporting to rely solely on logic, Frege's is entirely aprioristic in
character, though once a contradiction was detected in Frege's
system by Bertrand Russell, the argument ceased to be taken with
any great seriousness. By contrast, Quine's argument is fully
aposterioristic in some large-scale, holistic fashion, for his first
premiss (looking no further) is intended to express no more than
what just about any intelligent person might be expected to
believe who (a) respects the experimental results of modern science and (b) has lost confidence in any religious world-view. Such

a person will not be inclined to believe in abstract entities, and Quine was thus eager in his youth to join Nelson Goodman in a research project designed to eliminate them from the sciences.

The basic trick was supplied by Frege. Take the sentence 'Socrates has exactly two feet'. Let 'x is an F' stand for the predicate 'x is a foot of Socrates'. Then the sentence can be paraphrased as follows.

(4) $(\exists x)\,(\exists y)\,[x$ is an $F \cdot y$ is an $F \cdot \sim(x = y) \cdot (z)\,z$ is an $F \supset (z = x \times z = y)]$.

In the same vein, a sentence like 'There are exactly 9 planets in the solar system' can be replaced by another where the job done by '9' is now performed by our logical notation. Numbers as such simply drop out of consideration. However, these are merely the easy cases, where number words figure in a kind of adjectival capacity. It is when they appear in a substantival role that difficulties emerge, though even here a sentence like '9 is the exact number of the planets' can be taken to be a pretentious variant of the adjectival version. It is rather sentences like '9 is odd' and 'the exact number of planets is odd' that prove recalcitrant. Reluctantly conceding that the best that could be achieved along that line was the replacement of one sort of abstract entity—for example, numbers—by another, preferably sets, Quine felt in honour bound to declare himself a Platonist. An extraordinary event! That a scientist should tie his forthcoming theory to the results of an ongoing experiment in the laboratory was standard practice. But that a philosopher should be prepared to commit himself on the highest metaphysical level simply on the basis of this or that outcome of a research project was altogether unheard of; and it was his colleague Goodman who, by remaining intransigent in his anti-Platonism, proceeded in the familiar fashion of the so-called traditional philosopher with his *parti pris*. Even today one often hears it said that a philosopher's theory must needs rest ultimately on some more or less parochial 'intuition' to which he is wedded. Not so. Quine's example should suffice to show how, very much like the scientist, the metaphysician can propose a researchable hypothesis and bravely expose it to all the hazards of 'falsification'. No novelty, that procedure was recognized long ago by

Plato under the rubric of dialectic; though, over the centuries, no one has perhaps so vividly instantiated it as Quine.

Expressly tailored to suit the case of numbers, Quine's criterion of ontological commitment is hard pressed to accommodate the metaphysical relativist. Evidently one can have an ontology—that is, a theory of what it is to be—even though as a positive point of principle, more as a consequence of one's ontology, one refrains from taking on any ontological commitments whatever, as defined by Quine. No mere act of prudent self-denial, the decision of the relativist may be viewed as an outright affirmation of his nihilist convictions, and he may then be felt to qualify as a 'degenerate case' of ontological commitment. If Protagoras's wind, like everything else, fails to exist in itself, absolutely speaking, can it properly be said even to be self-identical? 'But surely,' someone may be inclined to protest, 'there is at least one thing that the wind must be allowed to be, absolutely speaking, namely a wind! Furthermore, that feature of the wind can only be regarded as an essential one.' No. Regarding the first claim, one has only to imagine a languid bug being wafted along by the wind who takes himself, naturally enough, to be buoyantly at rest in his ambience. Thus the bug might well be entitled to insist, relative to its life-world, that no wind could possibly be (blowing) in his immediate neighbourhood. As for the second claim, if 'the wind' is merely a mass of air in motion, then when it ceases to blow, it doubtless ceases to be a wind, but we need not say that it ceases to exist. If a soldier need not cease to exist merely because he ceases to be a soldier, there is room to doubt that the wind ceases to exist when it ceases to be a wind. Admittedly, the wind is a peculiar sort of entity, and the expression 'the wind', not to mention its 'blowing', may be still more deviant as a linguistic item.

Taken to be merely a mass of air, the wind can be admitted to our ontology only if, more generally, masses of air are to be so included. But how many masses of air are there, anyway? Overlapping entities of the most promiscuous kind, masses of air would appear to be peculiarly hard to count; and it is this feature of countability—to be is to be countable—that acquires normative authority under the auspices of Quine's criterion.

Thus one's hesitation as to whether the expression 'being *qua* being' contains two or three words may be resolved by distinguishing word-types from word-tokens; the formula instantiates two word-types even while it consists of three word-tokens.

This issue of number comes through most forcibly in connection with the very origins of philosophy. According to Aristotle the first philosophers were 'physicists', with Thales insisting that the fundamental substance was water, Anaximenes air, and Heraclitus fire. Accordingly, Nicholas White has suggested to me that (5) might be read as a recasting of Thales' ontology in Quinean terms, thus:

$$(5) \ (x) \ x \text{ is water.}$$

Testing the hypothesis, suppose we ask Thales whether in his opinion there are more or less than forty-six items in the universe, each of which consists entirely of water. For the issue of number is inescapable whenever we affirm in the Quinean manner that everything—that is, every x—is (an) F. On my hypothesis, Thales might be expected to reply with a laugh, 'But there is no number of things, absolutely speaking, though pragmatic considerations allow us to parcel out the world's water as it may suit our convenience, as we notice that here it is the more condensed, there the more rarefied. If on my theory there is only water and nothing else, that is not to be understood as entailing that there is either only one thing in the universe, which 'the world's water' might be supposed to denote, or that there are two or more things each of which consists solely of water.' In the same pre-Socratic vein someone today might be inclined to insist that there is only matter or only matter-energy, even while refusing to allow that there is either a finite or an infinite number of proper objects over which one is entitled to quantify in any absolute fashion. Although any such deviant ontology fails to satisfy Quine's criterion, I continue to cherish the criterion as an invaluable heuristic precisely because it enables us to identify non-standard as well as standard ontologies.

When it comes to standard ontologies, the most striking application of Quine's criterion is doubtless to be found in Donald Davidson's line of argument, which appeals directly to the resources of formal logic. Take the argument 'Tom is walking slowly; therefore Tom is walking'. Formally valid on the face of it, the argument might be supposed to invite the following rational reconstruction: 'Tom is walking and Tom is slow; therefore Tom is walking', where the abstract form of the argument is seen to be '$p \cdot q$', therefore p'. The trouble of course is that Tom may be walking slowly and at the same time talking quickly. As the relativist might observe, it is only relative to his walking that Tom is slow, not to his talking. But this slow walking and quick talking of Tom must then be recognized as two distinct events; accordingly, Davidson argues that we can hardly refrain from quantifying over events in our ontology once we concede that the argument ought to be represented as follows: $(\exists x)$ x is a walking $\cdot$ x is by Tom $\cdot$ x is slow; therefore $(\exists x)$ x is a walking $\cdot$ x is by Tom. If, hitherto, formal logic has scarcely ever been brought to bear on ontology with such immediate impact, no one today—least of all Davidson—supposes that the argument is decisive simply taken by itself alone, as if Thales in particular need feel threatened by it. I therefore look forward impatiently to Jonathan Bennett's forthcoming book on events that will canvass a wide range of collateral issues.

However much Davidson and Thales might appear to differ from each other, the one with his standard, the other with his non-standard ontology, they have this in common. The primary theme of ontology being found in the distinction between a thing and its properties, which logic comes to exploit on the basis of its grammatical counterpart—namely, the contrast between subject and predicate, on the linguistic level Davidson quite as much as Thales trades on a predicative anomaly. For it is the pesky role of the adverb in the predicate 'x is walking slowly' that the one undertakes to ontologize, and it is the deviance of the mass noun 'water' as it features in the predicate 'x is water'—compare it with the count noun 'dog' in 'x is a dog'—that the other turns to metaphysical account. There being no proper plural for substance terms like 'water', 'air', and 'gold', since, while there are many dogs, there is correspondingly only much gold, it was only to be expected that, with their mass-noun ontologies, the early pre-Socratics should be 'blind' to plurality, which is not to say, however, that the traditional characterization of them as monists, retrospectively pinned on them by the count-noun ontologists who came to dominate the field forever after, can be accepted by us as satisfactory.

Of the whole range of predicates, one emerges as the metaphysical predicate *par excellence*—namely, that of self-identity. And here again logic and ontology connect on the deepest level. For if the Tarskian balks at the very thought of everything's being self-identical, the Protagorean hesitates to allow that anything is so. Two accounts, one short, the other somewhat longer, can be given of Protagorean misgivings here. The short account exploits the 'fact' that existing and being self-identical come to pretty much the same thing. Because the relativist—and here, as always, I am thinking at least as much of the modern as of the classical variety—will not admit that anything can be said to exist *tout court*—that is, without qualification, absolutely speaking, *simpliciter*—he can hardly refrain from insisting on the same gamut of dialectical reservations when it comes to self-identity.

The longer account proceeds by way of a detour through Aristotle's doctrine of categories.

Part II

7
Categories

According to Aristotle, Protagorean relativism can be shown to be vitiated by what one can only call (following Gilbert Ryle) a category mistake. Specifically, Protagoras is accused of illicitly conflating the categories of substance and relation. Traditionally labelled also as 'predicaments', Aristotle's categories have been characterized by David Lachterman as styles of predication, and it is above all in connection with the categories that Aristotle writes, 'Being is said in many ways,' where those various ways of being, or of being *F*, are defined principally by the categories. The system of categories is precisely designed to classify and elucidate how the properties of a thing belong to it in their diversified ways.

Of Socrates one can say such things as (*a*) he is a man; (*b*) he is white; (*c*) he is more than 5 feet tall; (*d*) he is shorter than Plato; and (*e*) he is in Athens. If each answer is seen as answering the question 'What is Socrates?', one feels that although more than 5 feet tall is one thing Socrates is and white is another, it is only (*a*) that properly expresses *what he is*. To add that a further thing Socrates is, is in Athens, will almost certainly be received as the feeblest of witticisms. A man, white, more than 5 feet tall, shorter than Plato, in Athens: Socrates is, admittedly, all five of these things, though it might well be a source of puzzlement that one thing could also be five things. As a first stab at an answer, Aristotle says that Socrates is one of those five things primarily (*prôtôs*): namely, a man. The other four things he is only in some secondary or derivative fashion (*deuterôs, hupomenôs*). It is not to be supposed, however, that a man is the only thing that Socrates is primarily, or *simpliciter* (*haplôs*). An animal is another thing that Socrates is *simpliciter*. There is this difference, however, in *how* Socrates is those two things. Specifically a man, Socrates is an animal only generically speaking; and indeed this distinction between species and genus doubtless applies *mutatis mutandis* to the other categories as well. Man specifically and animal generically are predicated of Socrates under the category of substance; white specifically and (it may be) colour generically under the category of quality; being more than 5 feet tall specifically and (again maybe) having some height or other generically under the category of quantity; being a teacher of Plato specifically and . . . generically (I shan't even make a pretence at filling the gap) under the category of relation; being in Athens specifically and . . . generically under the category of place; and so forth as the Aristotelian schedule of categories—substance, quality, quantity, relation, action, passion, place, time, and so forth—appears to peter out inconsequentially.

Fairly perfunctory when it comes to the systematic elaboration of his scheme, Aristotle is content to appeal to the intuitive plausibility that attaches to his rough apparatus of classification, where the categories divide naturally into two principal classes. In the one class reposes substance in solitary splendour; in the other lie all the other categories. Even so, one feels that the former class may infinitely outweigh the latter. If being is said in many ways, it is said in two ways above all: namely, in the way of substance and in a non-substantial way. As Socrates in particular is primarily a man and only secondarily white, more than 5 feet tall, and the rest, so, more generally, what exists primarily is always a substance (for example, this cat, that dog) while every non-substantial item will be allowed to exist only *tropon tina*— that is, in a certain (apologetic) sort of way, in which each of the non-substantial categories (we are free to add the category of substance as a limiting case) may be said to constitute an ontological trope, to be contrasted with the traditional tropes of rhetoric. Both sorts of trope designate ways of being (something or other), the one literally, the other non-literally. Thus the rhetorical tropes of hyperbole and irony, as featured in 'That genius, Mr Toad!', serve to express one of the non-literal ways of being a genius.

When it comes to the literal ways of being (something or other), one is inclined to rebel at the thesis that here are two things that Socrates is: a man and more than 5 feet tall; and with Ryle one may suspect that a category mistake is being made, on a par with 'She came home in a flood of tears and a sedan-chair', which in fact is an example of the rhetorical trope of zeugma. A man, Socrates certainly is; but can he also be said to be, in the same literal sense of the word, more than 5 feet tall? Aristotle thinks not, and when he writes 'Being is said in many ways', he appears to be insisting that the word 'is' is equivocal as it undergoes a shift in its *literal* meaning when it is employed now in this, now in that category. Much less equivocal than 'bank' (as it pertains now to money, now to rivers), 'being' or 'is' functions specifically as a *pros hen*, or 'toward one', equivocal. Aristotle's favourite example of such an equivocal term is the word 'healthy', which, as predicated of food and (Thomas Aquinas's example) urine, as in 'healthy food' and 'healthy urine', signifies the kind of food or urine that in the one case *promotes* and in the other *indicates* health in the healthy animal; and it is in the expression 'healthy animal' that 'healthy' is predicated in its primary import, the other uses being secondary. Among the secondary uses of 'healthy' one may perhaps add 'a healthy mind', where the term is predicated by way of analogy. As all these secondary uses of 'healthy' are ordered *towards* the *one* primary use upon which each is seen to be parasitic, so every extra-substantial use of 'is' is understood by Aristotle to be parasitic on its primary application to substance. In the same vein, when it comes to giving the semantics of 'healthy', I should suppose that many philosophers today would prefer to assign it a secondary, as well as a primary, extension, the latter being a set limited to healthy animals, the former a set containing this food, that urine, and so on.

Compare now the awkward English of (1) with the regimented notation that is exhibited by (2):

(1) Socrates is both a man and more than 5 feet tall.
(2) $(\exists x)\, x$ is a man $\cdot$ x is more than 5 feet tall.

It is doubtless to be conceded that (1) at least smacks of zeugma, no such equivocation is present in (2), which can be abbreviated '$(\exists x)\, Fx \cdot Gx$' where a uniform notation simply rides roughshod over Aristotle's contrast between substantial and nonsubstantial predication. Thanks precisely to *his* logical approach to ontology, Quine accordingly insists that, appearances to the contrary, two different senses of 'is' are not being conflated in (1). Strikingly, however, Quine agrees with Aristotle that 'being— more exactly, the word 'is'—is shot through with ambiguity! At least since Bertrand Russell, one has routinely distinguished between the 'is' of predication (for example, 'Socrates is wise'), the 'is' of identity (for example, 'The Morning Star is the Evening Star'), and the 'is' of existence (for example, 'There is a cat under the bed)'. That the word 'is' has a different meaning in each case comes through most sharply when one considers that the second example can be paraphrased as 'The Morning Star is identical with the Evening Star', which features not the 'is' of identity but that of predication. This threefold ambiguity of 'is' proves now to be rendered completely unambiguous in our canonical notation, which proceeds to express each of the senses of 'is' by means of a distinct typographical device: ' = ', '$\exists x$', and 'Fx'.

The quarrel between Quine and Aristotle regarding (1) can now be seen to turn on only one of the three senses of 'is': namely, that of predication. This use of 'is', univocal for Quine, counts as itself equivocal for Aristotle. As a purely linguistic dispute regarding a mere word, the issue might readily be regarded as peripheral to the substantive issues of ontology. More generally, the case at hand provides an occasion for querying the whole 'linguistic turn', by which contemporary philosophers (so critics argue, Aristotle's example notwithstanding) have been badly sidetracked from their primary mission. Well, just look at how adjectives, adverbs, and mass nouns emerged for us as thematic in Chapter 6, though language as such is of no interest to us. Language connects with ontology only indirectly, through the mediation of logic, and it is already evident that in their dispute over (1), Aristotle is motivated principally by ontological consid- erations, Quine by logical ones if only because (1) entails (2) by existential generalization. Not that the 'is' of predication pro- vides the best arena for their encounter, given that in our own century (lest the issue should be felt to be factitiously anachronistic) Gilbert Ryle in the course of harking back to Aristotle's categories has not hesitated to plump for different senses of 'exist'. Existence being for Quine precisely what the existential quantifier of logic univocally expresses, this neo-Aristotelian position of Ryle he finds still more unacceptable.

How the putative ambiguity of the word 'exist' can be brought to bear on a substantive issue of ontology, Ryle illustrates above all in his effort to overcome the dualism of mind and body that has been so characteristic of modern philosophy ever since Descartes in the seventeenth century. Adopting a behaviourist or quasi-behaviourist approach to mind, Ryle argues in effect that to say there are minds as well as bodies commits one to the category mistake of supposing that in addition to each human being there is also his behaviour, as if two entities were involved. Behaviour in fact reminds us of two minor categories in Aristotle's scheme: namely, action and passion. When we say, 'Socrates is walking', walking is predicated of Socrates in the category of action. More fundamental than actual behaviour in Ryle's theory of mind is our whole range of dispositions to behave in various ways in different circumstances. All such dispositions to behave presuppose in us various potentialities; indeed, when Aristotle writes, 'Being is said in many ways', he is thinking not only of his categorial scheme, but also of the distinction between actual and potential being which is re-enacted afresh in each of the categories. Again, for Aristotle, to be as such is always to be actual (in the category of substance), since potential being is regarded as a sort of non-being. For if an acorn is potentially an oak tree, it is a fortiori not an oak tree, that is to say, it is not actually an oak tree, which proves that to be (an) *F simpliciter* is always to be actually (an) *F*. To say now that there is potential, as well as actual, being is to be guilty of a category mistake in Ryle's, though not Aristotle's, terminology; in the same vein, 'there are dogs and there are animals' must be faulted for being 'categorially' confused through failure to respect the difference in 'logical type' between species-words and genus-words. Because mind connects above all with dispositions to behave, which in their turn connect with potentialities, to say that there is mind as well as body involves at least two category mistakes, one featuring the categories of substance and action, the other those of actuality and potentiality.

Up to this point in his critique of Cartesian mind–body dualism, Ryle can probably be said to be at least broadly in

accord with Quine and Aristotle alike, on the particular issue.
Quine breaks with Ryle, however, when Ryle urges that while one
is entitled 'to say in one logical tone of voice that there exist
minds' as well as 'to say in another tone of voice that there exist
bodies', it must be understood that 'these expressions . . . indicate two different senses of "exist" ', which one conflates at
one's peril if one should dare to add that 'there exist both minds
and bodies'. In fact, 'it would be just as good or bad a joke to say
that there exist prime numbers and Wednesdays and public opinion and navies'.[1] Ironically enough, the joke vividly expresses
what Quine in all seriousness takes to be involved in ontological
commitment. Our reluctance to quantify over Wednesdays in our
ontology, even though we can be heard on occasion to remark
that they are especially tedious through being so remote from the
weekend, Quine is fully prepared to respect. Months and Wednesdays being on a par as intervals of time, it is not to be supposed
that we can acknowledge only some of them on a piecemeal basis.
Taken as a package, they presumably comprise infinitely many
items, some of which are $\sqrt{2}$ minutes long, and if temporal, why
not spatial intervals as well?

A Quinean riposte to Ryle can now be framed as follows. If
only because the reality of the philosopher's seminar room consists first and foremost of tables and chairs, it is to be expected
that such medium-sized dry goods should be felt to enjoy some
sort of primacy when it comes to the furniture of the world. By
contrast, spatial and temporal intervals are precisely the sort
of 'ghostly' items—minds, events and numbers are others—that
metaphysical controversy thrives upon, and Occam's razor is
always ready at hand to give reality a close shave by removing
them. Scarcely daring to deny their existence outright, however,
the philosopher has every incentive to 'fudge' the issue. Why not
say, then, that while failing to exist in the primary sense of the
word, such items do exist in some secondary sense, though one
will doubtless blush when it comes to positing a third, omnibus
sense of the word so as to accommodate '$(\exists x) x = x$'. The trouble
of course is that in sharp contrast to 'bank', where the different

---

[1] G. Ryle, *The Concept of Mind* (London: Hutchinson, 1949), p. 23.

senses of the word can be readily specified by the professional linguist, no such distinction for the word 'exist' is available.

Particularly disturbing for us in these pages is the emergence of Aristotle as an ally of Wittgenstein, Tarski, and Protagoras in their diversified rejection of the Principle of Identity. Expressly denying that 'being is a genus' that encompasses everything whatever, be it a substantial or a non-substantial item, Aristotle seems bent on convicting us of metaphysical zeugma when we insist that everything without exception, non-substantial as well as substantial, *is* identical with itself. Which sense of 'is' are you invoking here, I can hear him asking; for he will not allow a trans-categorial sense that ranges indifferently over all the categories.

8

Relations

On at least one occasion Aristotle remarks that some non-substantial categories are more substance-like, or more akin to substance, than others. In particular, quality is more substantial, as we might say, than quantity, and quantity in its turn is more substantial than relation. How one might be inclined as an empiricist like John Locke to identify primary reality with the observable qualities of things rather than the things themselves, Aristotle is prepared to understand; and that a mathematical physicist like Newton should suggest that bodies might be defined as 'determinate quantities of extension' he would not find surprising, bearing in mind that Aristotle takes mathematics to be the theory of quantity or magnitude, both discrete (arithmetic) and continuous (geometry). In both cases we are sticking fairly close to the thing itself. When it comes to Protagoras, however, his tolerance can only terminate abruptly. Simply too far down the line, the category of relation, precisely by being engaged in relating one thing to another, can only lead us away from the thing itself. When the perceptual (and conceptual) relativist insists that to be as such is to be relative (no matter to what), he is guilty of passing the metaphysical buck.

The case of self-identity can now be seen to be of the greatest interest. For if the predicate 'x is identical with y' counts in logic as a relational expression, the relational or pseudo-relational property expressed by the predicate can hardly be said to lead us away from one thing to another. Although the predicate does undertake to do just that in the sentence 'London is identical with Paris', it expressly denies that it is doing so; hence the falsity. One might be inclined to say that identity—that is, self-identity—is the great exception among relations, being the only one that a thing can bear to itself. Not so. The relation 'x is exactly as large as y' is only one of infinitely many so-called reflexive relations that this page bears to itself, and there is one such relation that pertains especially to Protagoras's wind: namely, 'x is exactly as cold (or hot as the case may be) as y.' Because the wind, though cold to me, is not cold to you, Protagoras takes it to be in itself neither cold nor not cold. Accordingly, I very much doubt that he can allow the wind to be exactly as cold as itself. There is indeed some question as to how we are to treat '6 is exactly as cold as 7'. If Ryle would rule it out of bounds as being vitiated by a category mistake, Quine, with whom my own sympathies lie, would wish to assign it a truth value. Seeing that 6 and 7 are definitely not cold, they may be allowed in a degenerate sort of way to be each exactly *as* cold as the other—that is, not cold at all. A limiting case of thermal parity being acknowledged here, Protagoras's wind cannot be supposed to satisfy the predicate 'x is exactly as cold as x' in the same manner, and there is no logical room left over beyond the limit. Every reflexive relation that a thing is presumed to bear to itself, Protagoras must view with the keenest suspicion. Precisely to attend to a thing in its relatedness to itself alone, whether in this or in that respect, involves attending to the thing as it is on its own; but no such thing on its own exists, according to Protagoras.

That this page *is* exactly as large as itself, being a self-evident truth, might be thought to refute Protagoras outright. I do not believe it. It may be enough here merely to glance at the famous dispute between Newton and Leibniz regarding the ontology of space (and place), where the one insists that space is absolute, the other that it is relative. Imagine a universe that contains nothing but a single apple. Can we further suppose the apple to be moving in a figure of 8? Yes, of course, says Newton. No, says Leibniz, who will not even allow the apple to be at rest, for to be at rest is simply to remain in the same place, and if that were possible it would be no less possible for the apple to vacate its place and occupy another. Strictly speaking, on Leibniz's admittedly counter-intuitive view, there are no antecedent places available for the apple to occupy or to fail to occupy. The apple is thus nowhere! An anti-realist with respect to place and space (and size), the relativist is widely regarded as being on especially strong ground when he insists that an object can be properly said to be moving (or at rest) only relative to this or that further object, for even the anti-relativist has hesitated to contest the point. Having remarked as early as chapter 2 that no philosopher has failed to be a relativist about something, I can now adduce the present issue as one where philosophers are especially prone to go relativist if only because physics would appear to have decided the issue. More recently, however, spatial absolutism has been reactivated. Suppose, with Einstein, that space is non-Euclidean, and in particular that it is Riemannian—that is, *finite* but unbounded—then, in these still more counter-intuitive circumstances, space as a whole might be thought to have a definite size or magnitude of its own.

If so minor a category in the Aristotelian scheme as that of place can pose such vexing issues, it is only to be expected that each of the major categories should constitute a whole branch of metaphysics; and when it comes specifically to metaphysical relativism, the category of relation cannot but pre-empt attention. Because even the metaphysical absolutist, who may well be a Leibnizean relativist regarding space, can feel uneasy over the reflexive predicate '*x* is exactly as large as *x*', Protagoras must be acquitted of any special embarrassment in that respect. Absolutist and relativist separate when it comes to the identity predicate, though even here a surprising affinity between them emerges. With the thesis that to be as such is to be relative, the absolutist is found suddenly to concur. The whole issue turns on *what* it might be that a thing is supposed to be relative *to*. Why not itself? It is precisely that sort of relatedness that divides the absolutist from the relativist, as the former undertakes to see the latter hoist with his own petard. Engaged in no mere dialectical skirmish improvised for the occasion, the logical absolutist, as we may style him, has been antecedently motivated to express the proposition that there is something not nothing in the following notation:

$$(1) \quad (\exists x)\, x = x.$$

If existence is fully expressed by the existential quantifier, how explain the need here to eke it out with the identity predicate? Why not simply abbreviate (1) to $(\exists x)$? Is that not to be read as 'there exists an x, namely something'? No. Much more perspicuous for our purposes is:

$$(2)\ (\Sigma x)\ (x = x),$$

which is standardly taken to be the merest notational variant of (1), though (2) is naturally read as meaning that something (or some x) is identical with itself. Abbreviating (2) to 'Σx' would thus yield the sentence fragment 'Some x' or 'Something' or at best 'Something is . . .', where the 'is' is the 'is' of predication, not existence. In (2), existence (or a facsimile thereof) appears to be fully expressed by the predicate! In the teeth of Aristotle's denigration of the whole category of relation, there proves to be one relation that the logical absolutist of today singles out as metaphysically privileged. To be, then, is to be self-related, above all, to be self-related in the mode of identity.

Lest it be supposed that any principle to the effect that to be is to be . . . (fill the blank as you choose) must involve a vicious circle, since the word 'be' is used twice over, one need only recall the threefold ambiguity of 'is'. The formula 'to be is to be . . .' is thus to be rendered unambiguous by noticing that the first 'is' is the 'is' of existence, while the second is that of predication. As for the third 'is', that of identity, the formula 'to be is to be self-identical' enjoys a peculiar felicity in that, while only the first and second 'is' appear therein, what the third 'is' expresses, namely being identical with something or other, is what the formula positively features. Maybe, then, what it is to exist ought to be explained less in the specific terms of being *self*-identical than in the more general terms of being identical with something or other. Explained? Contrary to my own sentiments, most philosophers feel that at this bedrock level the whole notion of explanation simply fails to apply. How, indeed, explain what it is to exist, as if there were something at once more intelligible and more fundamental? I shall not linger here to argue the point, being content to note that only after one has in hand an adequate account of explanation as such—again the 'as such'—can one pronounce on the issue with much authority. Protagoras certainly addresses being as such, but the terms in which he undertakes to elucidate it remain themselves unexamined. Now that the relational (the relational as such) has emerged as itself thematic, against the dual background of Aristotle's categorial scheme and Frege's logic, the dialectic of absolute and relative takes an unexpected turn, which Hegel is entitled to relish.

We begin with being as such, understood in terms of the thing in itself, for, as Michael Dummett observes, 'how things are in themselves is . . . the fundamental question of metaphysics.' Antithetical to the absolutist thesis is the insistence that nothing exists in itself but only relative to . . ., and here the perceptual and conceptual relativist fill the blank each in his own way. How, precisely, may a thing be related to itself, the absolutist is now prompted to ask in the face of the relativist's challenge. Thesis and antithesis being taken to read, respectively, 'To be is to be absolute' and 'To be is to be relative', the synthesis that transcends the opposition: namely, 'To be is to be self-related'— vindicates the *content* of the thesis, even while it takes the *form* principally of the antithesis. Alienated from one another in formal logic (as we noticed in Chapter 4), form and content are here reconciled. Not relatedness in general, however, but only one particular mode of relatedness—namely, self-relatedness, and, more particularly still, self-identity—is found to be what constitutes absolute being. A gnomic utterance characteristic of metaphysics conducted in the grand style, the pronouncement may be securely registered as follows for future reference.

(3) To be is to be absolute, where absolute being consists in self-relatedness generically and in self-identity specifically.

Admittedly rebarbative, (3) might well be regarded as the sort of woolly dictum with which Hegel's *Logic* abounds on page after page. A little of Hegel goes a long way, and there need be no fear that I shall more than dabble in his idiom. If in retrospect Hegel and Frege appear to be the major philosophers of the nineteenth century, their striking incongruity has been thought to be altogether recalcitrant to any systematic integration of their approaches, and this rift warrants our agreeing with Heidegger when he speaks of the nineteenth as 'this most ambiguous century'. Failure to grasp coherently our own immediate antecedents in the past century may not be without peril to our 'pure philosophizing' today. As a pure metaphysical thesis in the most contentious sense of the term, (3) is scarcely intelligible apart from a logico-metaphysical framework that accommodates Hegel and Frege with almost equal facility.

Waiving all merely dialectical considerations, at the heart of (3) lies a salient fact: namely, that when absolute and relative are contrasted as *co*-relative, an independent, antecedent science pertains to one of the two, whereas nothing comparable can be found in the case of the other. Having identitifed the relative with the relational, it should be noticed that we have firmly in hand, after Frege, an abstract science of relations which allows for a one-way elucidation, if not an 'explanation', of the absolute—that is, *per se* existence, in its precise terms. At the core of the new logic lies the n-place predicate, which expresses an n-place relation. Beginning with the monadic, or 1-place, predicate—for example, 'x is wise'—one proceeds to the dyadic, or 2-place, predicate—for example, 'x is larger than y'—then the triadic—for example, 'x is between y and z'—and so on. Equivalence relations prove to be of special interest to us, being at once reflexive, symmetric, and transitive in their inferential powers. Although transitive, owing to (4) below, 'larger than' is found to be both anti-reflexive and anti-symmetric, owing to (5) and (6), whereas 'x loves y' is merely non-reflexive and non-symmetric, owing to (7) and (8).

(4) (x) (y) (z) x is larger than y · y is larger than $z \supset x$ is larger than z.

(5) (x) $\sim$ (x is larger than x).

(6) (x) (y) (x is larger than y) $\supset \sim$ (y is larger than x).

(7) $\sim (x)$ x loves x.

(8) $\sim [(x)$ (y) x loves $y \supset y$ loves $x]$.

Intuitively, one is invited to consider every equivalence relation as featuring a kind of identity. For if x is exactly as witty as y, they may perhaps be said to be identical with one another with respect to wittiness. Or, if one prefers, one may have recourse to a trope known technically as 'abstraction', and say that the degree of wittiness to be found in x is identical with the degree of wittiness to be found in y. How the logic of relations provides 'the money in the bank' in support of our Hegelian principle, as (3) may be designated, should be fairly evident, though there is an inevitable irony in our undertaking to vindicate the absolute by appealing to the science of relations, as if primacy were to be accorded to the category of relation, rather than that of substance. In fact, by allowing that absolute and relative are co-*relative* notions precisely in virtue of their *différance* (invoking the idiolect of Jacques Derrida) as polar opposites, I might even be charged with having allowed the relativist to deconstruct the absolute.

The immediate relevance of (3) to Protagoras's specific line of argument may be brought out as follows. Let it be granted that this table, while cool and smooth to our touch, is warm and rough to that of the Martians. Suppose it further to be heavy to us, light to them, brown to us, blue to them, rectangular to us, round to them. Let it even be a table only to us but a battering-ram in hand-to-hand combat for them, though we may concede to Protagoras that really relevant here are only the sensible qualities in the narrow sense. Even conceding so much, we must insist that Protagoras's conclusion—namely, that nothing exists in itself— is premature. The most that follows is a doctrine that may be styled 'predicate relativism', which even requires a subject absolutism. Socrates may be intimating as much when somewhat awkwardly he says that 'sometimes when the *same* wind blows one of us feels cold and the other does not'. Even so, we must guard against the case where the part of the wind to which you are exposed is really much warmer than the part bearing down on me. Only if the thing that is cold or whatever to me is precisely identical with the thing that is not cold or whatever to you, can Protagoras launch his argument, but once that common ground is acknowledged, it is seen to be the thing in itself that exists absolutely speaking.

9

Functions

Very much on the way *to* first principles in these pages, we cannot
but feel the need to reassure ourselves that we have some understanding of what it would be like to achieve our goal. The
Hegelian principle comes to sight as precisely the sort of proposition in which metaphysics executed in the grand manner may be
expected to terminate. What its vindication might consist in, we
already know, at least in part. For at its core lies the Principle of
Identity, which one logician described recently as being 'according to taste . . . either the supreme metaphysical truth or the
utmost banality',[1] and which has been found to elicit a bewil-
dering battery of misgivings that reach all the way from
Wittgenstein to Aristotle. Daunted by the prospect of undertaking to allay those misgivings on any one-on-one basis, I am
reminded anew of Plato's insistence that knowledge absolute on
the highest level of the Divided Line requires that one be able to
run the gauntlet of all objections.[2] That nothing less than a *theory*
exercising a synoptic command over all the relevant data, empirical as well as logical, could possibly empower one to run the
dialectical gauntlet successfully, let it only be in defence of the
Principle of Identity, one can hardly be expected to doubt.

After all the others, Frege's reservations about the Principle
come now as a particular surprise, if only because 'it was Frege',
writes Dummett, 'who first made identity a logical notion',
enshrining it above all in the formula '$(x)\,x = x$'. The difficulty is
that the formula is taken by Frege to say merely that every *object*
is identical with itself, and that not quite everything is an object
for Frege. How these non-objectual items, none of which is
capable of being assigned a proper name even by God and to
which the concept of identity fails properly to apply, are to be

---

[1] Wilfrid Hodges, *Logic* (Harmondsworth: Penguin Books, 1977), p. 164.
[2] Plato, *Republic*, vii. 543C.

accommodated in our thinking proves to be quite as mystifying as any topic in the metaphysical canon. At the end of his paper 'Function and Concept', Frege insists that these items are 'founded deep in the nature of things', though any elucidation of them, particularly as they contrast with objects, could hardly be expected to dispense with 'metaphors' and 'hints', as he remarks at the end of his paper 'Concept and Object'. One is struck above all by the way in which it is precisely in his capacity as foundational logician that Frege turns by default to metaphor in his effort to explain these 'unsaturated' or 'incomplete' items that are founded deep in the nature of things. What, then, are these deviant items to which the Principle of Identity fails to apply? In a word, they are functions in the mathematician's sense of the term, though that answer can serve only as a first approximation. They are at any rate function-like, and at least something 'analogous' (Frege's word) to identity applies to them. A professional mathematician, Frege is to be seen as drawing on a treasured resource of his discipline in a highly intuitive effort to apply it to the ontological underpinnings of logic.

The prospect of enriching philosophy with the resources of mathematics, long regarded as involving the purest and most successful exercise of rationality, has inevitably tantalized philosophers ever since Plato, though it was not until Frege that one had much of a notion as to how the vision was to be implemented. In our own search for first principles, we are in need of all the help we can get, and thus the opportunity to draw on mathematics can hardly fail to be exhilarating. At the very least the range of considerations available to us in the long haul will be enlarged, thereby enabling us more nearly to fulfil our holistic ambitions.

Functions in particular come into play on the most elementary level of Frege's logic, even before the quantifiers (universal and existential) have been introduced, when we are content merely to mind our p's and q's. Recalling Chapter 5, in which we discussed the truth conditions for statements of the form '$p \times q$', we are soon found to be conjuring with the idiom of functions when we are heard to say, 'The truth value of any statement with the form "$p \times q$" is a function of the truth values assigned to p and q respectively,' meaning no more than that the supervenient truth or falsity of '$p \times q$' depends entirely on the precise 'mix' of truth and falsity antecedently acquired by p and q taken separately, and it is thus the truth table that exhibits this relation of dependency in the most graphic fashion. If, when it comes to this elementary, so-called truth-functional logic, the jargon of functions might well appear to be the merest window-dressing, later it can be seen to carry metaphysical import with the advance to so-called quantificational or predicate logic. Not that the notion of a function, even on its own home ground in straight mathematics, is taken by Frege to be a fully determinate matter, for in its elasticity it must be recognized as having undergone an ever-increasing enlargement of scope over the previous two centuries. The paradigm case is doubtless to be found in the continuous function, as when the length of a tree's shadow is said to be a function of the tree's height, where answering to any minute increase in the latter will be a correspondingly minute increase in the former, by way of concomitant variation. One variable quantity's answering to another in some systematic fashion appears to be the underlying thought. Impoverished in comparison with continuous magnitudes, discrete ones are later found also to admit of functions, as when sticking to the domain of natural numbers we say that 7 is a function of 6, having in mind the successor function $f(x) = x + 1$. Which is not to say that 7 really is a function, let alone a function *of* something. If the informal idiom here is confessedly defective, Dummett may well be right when he urges that the very notion of a function is inescapably bound with it. Apart from such standard functions as $g(x) = 6x^3 + 5x^2 - 98$ that takes 3 as argument to yield 109 as the value of the function for that argument, that is, $g(3) = 109$, there is the constant function, for example $h(x) = 12$, that takes every number into 12 (or whatever). Especially dear to the metaphysician must be the identity function that takes everything into itself.

If the identity and constant functions open the way for the first time to the use of function theory outside mathematics, within the science proper there remains the so-called characteristic function of Dirichlet that more than any other came to shape Frege's enterprise. While correlating each rational in the domain of the real numbers with 1, the characteristic function assigns each irrational to 0, though London and Paris could serve almost equally well as the respective values of the function for each rational and irrational argument. I say 'almost' because the suggestion is that 1 and 0 enjoy a certain mythical appropriateness, the one in affirming, the other in denying, that some item possesses the characteristic of being a rational number. Better still, one would like to assign each rational to yes and each irrational to no if only 'yes' and 'no' could be taken to denote entities. Already in Dirichlet, then, function theory can be seen to be straining at the leash, ready to take off on its own, as all the characteristics of things, non-mathematical as well as mathematical, promise to be expressible in terms of functions. Ascribing a characteristic to a thing having long been recognized as what predication is all about, Frege's move, as a mathematical logician, can come to seem virtually inevitable. The thought that Socrates is wise features the characteristic function $w(x) = 1$ if x is wise while $w(x) = 0$ if x is not wise, though the use of 1 and 0 here as the respective values of the wisdom function has much too stipulatory a character to satisfy the classic purity of a mind like Frege's. For what we are seeking is always the truth, and indeed it can be seen that the thought that Socrates is wise presents us with the truth, as every true thought presents us with the truth even in those cases where, ignorant of the fact that the thought is a true thought, we fail to realize that it is the truth and not falsity with which the thought presents us.

Taken on its own, the previous sentence is likely to be passed over as an upholstered banality when in fact it must be read literally as expressing some of Frege's most perplexing views. If only for systematic reasons the value of the wisdom function for Socrates taken as argument turns out to be indeed a *truth* value—namely, a certain object that one may variously designate as 'the truth', 'the true', or even simply 'truth', as now one, now another of these expressions strikes one as appropriate. That there really is any such single object as the truth, almost no philosopher is prepared to take seriously, though we are inconsistent enough to bandy with truth values when it comes to logic and semantics, and it is not to be doubted that any such expression as 'the truth value of the sentence "Socrates is wise"' must be taken grammatically to be a definite description that, like any singular term, professes to pick out an object. Both informally, then, as when we say that we are seeking the truth, and in the regimented jargon of semantics we are virtually advertising ourselves as Fregeans in respect to truth. Why not then simply allay all scepticism here by pressing into service the property of being true (possessed by certain beliefs and sentences) with which we are already on familiar enough terms? Let w(Socrates) = the property of being true.

It turns out, however, that the whole point of Frege's functional account of predication lies in its allowing us to dispense with all properties across the board. To begin with, altogether traditional in his approach to predication, Frege takes the basic sentence 'Socrates is wise' to feature a concept as well as an object, where the object is Socrates himself and the concept supplies the content of the predicate 'x is wise'. If the concept in its turn is identified by Frege with a characteristic function, that might be supposed—mistakenly—to be no more than a mathematician's way of handling properties under another name. In fact what is positively constitutive of functions proves to be their failure to satisfy Quine's maxim 'No entity without identity'. How questions of identity (and diversity) might be felt to lapse in the case of equivalent functions, one can understand readily enough. Thus, consider the 'planet' function, namely $p(x) = x + 10 - c$, where c = the number of planets. Is the 'planet' function (identical with) the successor function? Well, they are certainly equi-valent—that is, equal-valued—for they always have the same value for the same argument, given any argument whatever. Or consider the mermaid and the centaur functions that map everything into the second truth value—namely, falsity. Although the concepts that supply the content of the predicates 'x is a mermaid' and 'x is a centaur' one standardly supposes to be different concepts, just as the corresponding properties are almost as often taken to be different, it is much less clear how one is to regard the relevant functions, given that their schedules of correlation are indistinguishable. If the tendency today is on the side of identifying each function with its correlation schedule, no such consensus solidified in Frege's time, and even today one may be entitled to argue that when it comes to equivalent functions God himself cannot determine whether they are identical. Misgivings regarding Quine's maxim, let alone the Principle of Identity, need not be involved here at all. One may prefer to regard functions as provisional items, proprietary to the mathematical sciences, whose (relative) indeterminacy is entirely suited to the limited purposes for which they are designed. One may then insist with Quine on tight criteria of identity and diversity only when it comes to the demands of ontology proper.

But no such eirenic approach could possibly satisfy Frege, who might be expected to reply as follows: 'Just like a philosopher! Ever since Plato, the philosopher has flattered himself on attaining a level of cognition by comparison with which the mere mathematician can qualify only as a kind of second-best. Please be not offended if I content myself with the limited understanding to which my science affords me access.'

10

Predication

Apart from my interest in Frege's functions in their threatening role as putative counter-examples to the Principle of Identity, in his pages quite as much as in Aristotle's, the theory of predication can be seen to emerge in its own right as integral to the whole logico-ontological enterprise; witness Butchvarov's recent *Being qua Being*, with its suggestive subtitle *A Theory of Existence, Identity and Predication*, which undertakes to encompass the threefold ambiguity of 'is' in a unitary vision. There is, however, an evident difficulty. A unitary vision of what? Of being itself— that is, being *qua* being—one is tempted to reply, as if there were some fourth super-sense of 'is' under which the other three senses of existence, identity, and predication might be subsumed as the three species of an overarching genus; which is doubtless absurd. In fact a theory of being might well be felt to be on all fours with a theory of banks that is addressed to a domain consisting solely of river banks and money banks. The trouble, of course, is that there is no third, neutral sense of 'bank' that enables one to say that river banks and money banks are both banks, and by parity of reasoning it has been argued that traditional ontology with its conceit of a theory of being as such is infected with the same confusion when it postulates a spurious super-sense to the word 'being'.

The readiest response to the charge lies in the recognition already mentioned that the theory of being as such is none other than the theory of existence, where, however, what it is to exist proves to be scarcely distinguishable from what it is to be self-identical; thus, being self-identical, if it features one predicate among all others, also puts the issue of predication as such squarely in our lap. For predicative being—that is, being *F*—now turns out to be a genus of which existence—that is, just plain being or being *tout court*—is a species in the predicative mode of being self-identical. Generically speaking to be understood in terms of what the 'is' of predication expresses, existence is to be understood more specifically in terms of what the 'is' of identity expresses. As the theory of what the 'is' of existence expresses, ontology turns out to be precisely the theory of what the 'is' of predication and the 'is' of identity express, the one generically, the other specifically. That the theory of anything whatever involves *specifying* what the thing is in terms of something more *general*, one recalls at once as standard Aristotelian doctrine regarding species and genus, and ontology must thus address this whole issue of generality and specificity in its theory of predication.

Although one is now likely to have the eerie feeling that the threefold, ostensible ambiguity of the word 'is' is a mere surface phenomenon that we have succeeded in dispelling, that feeling must be resisted as itself an illusion. As a point of straight linguistics, 'is' remains as equivocal as ever, but, like any proper inquiry, ontology is to be seen as addressed to one thing, not three things. That one thing can be identified quite apart from the linguistic vagaries of the word 'is'. Concerned in general with what is involved in being F (for any F), ontology is concerned in particular with being self-identical—that is to say, with existing. How precisely the adventitious quirks associated with the word 'is' connect with the ontological enterprise so understood (the threefold nexus having been disentangled) can now be dismissed as the merest distraction, and one may well feel entitled to rely henceforth on the purified notation of the new logic. Even here, however, fine points of language, if not outright ambiguity, have their part to play, as the following formulae attest:

$$(1) \quad (\exists x)\,(x = x).$$
$$(2) \quad (\Sigma x)\,(x = x).$$
$$(3) \quad (\Sigma x)\,(\Sigma y)\ x = y.$$
$$(4) \quad (\exists F)\,(x)\ Fx.$$
$$(5) \quad (\Sigma x)\,(\Sigma F)\ Fx.$$

Although (2) is standardly considered to be the merest stylistic variant of (1), the difference is not quite negligible. Where (1) is naturally read as 'There exists an x such that x is identical with x',

(2) reads, 'Some *x* is identical with *x*', or even simply 'Something is identical with itself'. If in strict logic there is no difference between the so-called existential and the so-called particular quantifier, the provenance of the latter in traditional logic is worth recalling, by way of the distinction between universal and particular propositions: for example, 'All men are mortal' versus 'Some men are mortal'. Why I have come to prefer (2) to (1) as a way of saying that something and not nothing exists should be fairly evident. Sticking to (1), I was forced in effect to concede that if existence is expressed therein by the identity predicate, it is equally, and redundantly, expressed by the quantifier as well, suggesting in fact that when it comes to expressing existence quantifier and predicate must be allowed to divide the honours. With (2) I am home free. The quantifier merely contributes the word 'something', while the existence of the thing is secured entirely by the predicate. Mere sleight of hand? Perhaps. Consider, however, the powerful impression that I am undertaking to dispel, an impression jointly implanted by two independent factors. On the one hand, there is Kant's famous critique of Anselm's Ontological Argument, in which he insists in a negative vein that existence—actually he uses the word 'being'—is not a real predicate, leaving one perplexed as to what it might be. On the other hand, there is the positive doctrine of recent years: namely, that existence is in fact what the existential quantifier of modern logic expresses, which not only confirms Kant's position (how could a predicate be confused with a quantifier?) but even fills the Kantian void. Between the two, one is left with the sense of an unbridgeable gulf separating what is expressed by the 'is' of existence from what is expressed by the 'is' of predication, when in fact the former is merely a species of the latter.

If I prefer (2) to (1) precisely because it exhibits existence, or at any rate a surrogate of existence, as a real predicate, I have come in turn to prefer (3) over (2), if for less weighty reasons. Pedantically read as 'Some *x* is identical with some *y*', (3) may be taken to say that something is identical with something, where the suggestion that two things may be involved is actually to be welcomed, granted that it is speedily erased. Recalling my earlier suggestion that to be—that is, to exist—is to be understood less in

terms of being self-identical than in terms of being identical with
something or other, we see that (3) harbours the thought that
what it is for something to exist is for it to be identical with
something, let that something be anything whatever. The reflex-
ivity of the identity relation, while evident enough, need no more
be stressed here than the fact of its being transitive and
symmetric.

If to be is to be (identical with) something, it turns out also to
be the case that to be is to be something in a very different sense of
the words 'is' and 'something' that recalls a wayward idiom of
which I availed myself—much too cavalierly, I fear—in Chapter
7 where more than 5 feet tall was one thing Socrates was found to
be, wise another. It is precisely in that vein that to be (exist) is to
be something—for example, more than 5 feet tall, wise, self-
identical, shorter than Plato, in Athens, a man. Although the
second use of 'be' here would seem to be largely predicative in
import, the deviant use of 'something' requires special attention,
even beckoning us towards the hermeneutics of second-order
logic that features such formulae as (4), routinely read as 'There
exists a certain property F such that everything is F.' Quine
deplores this sentence as scarcely grammatical, on the ground
that it confuses F as a mere dummy expression, or 'substitution-
taking schematic letter', with 'a value-taking variable', the first
'F' in the sentence serving in the latter capacity, the second in the
former. Grammaticality aside, Quine assures us that if quantifying over properties is to be taken as the specific mission of
second-order logic, the task can be readily performed by first-
order predicate logic on its own, as by the following:

(6) $(\exists x)$ x is a property · (y) y has x.

Arguably, the ultimate refinement in contemporary philosophy
is to be found among those logicians who, even while they eschew
second-order logic as a device for quantifying over properties,
cherish it for a very different, Fregean sort of reason. The trick
here is to draw on the wayward idiom of our vulgar tongue (as I
am prepared to style it in a spirit of blatant tendentiousness) in
order to gloss (4) as 'There is something that everything is'. In
that same vein (5) is to be read as 'Something is something', but

not in the way that (3) says that something is (identical with) something. Serving as the particular quantifier, 'something' is now found to operate very differently, maybe even equivocally, as between its second-order and first-order roles. The difference comes out most vividly in connection with Dummett's sample sentence 'There is something George has never learned how to use.' What might that be? Well, 'a motor mower'.

> If I now press further and ask, 'Which motor mower has George never learned how to use?', it is just possible that I might be told, 'The one he keeps borrowing from his neighbour—he can manage others all right'— in which case the speaker was using 'something' in the original sentence to express first-level generality: but the probability is that my question will be rejected as displaying a misunderstanding.[1]

Detachability in the one case but not the other can be seen to be a formal feature that distinguishes first-order use of 'something' from second-order use, as the following pseudo-argument indicates:

(7) More than 5 feet tall is something which Socrates and Plato both are.

Therefore,

(8) More than 5 feet tall is something.

If '(7) therefore (8)' is saved from being an invalid argument, it is only thanks to the fact that the detachment of (8) from (7) fails to yield a proper sentence, at any rate when (8) undertakes to retain the sense it has in (7). For (8) can of course be read as a (barely) acceptable inversion of (9):

(9) $(\exists x)\, x$ is more than 5 feet tall.

A better example for our purpose is given by (10), (11), and (12).

(10) A centaur is something that neither Socrates nor Plato is.

Therefore,

(11) A centaur is something.

---

[1] M. Dummett, *Frege: Philosophy of Language*, 2nd edn. (Cambridge, Mass.: Harvard University Press, 1981), p. 68.

Therefore,

(12) $(\exists x)$ x is a centaur.

On being detached from (10), (11) can stand by itself as a complete sentence only if it retreats from its second-order to a first-
order reading. Invested with second-order import, (11) is found
to be inherently incomplete as a mere fragment of a sentence, and
it is precisely this incompleteness—translated now from language
to reality—that appears to explain Frege's conviction that while
each of the expressions 'more than 5 feet tall' and 'a centaur', as
they appear in (7) and (10), refers to something, the something
that each refers to is 'unsaturated' or 'incomplete', as he chooses
to put it in the mode of metaphor.

   In a spirit at once Fregean and Aristotelean one would like to
assert (13):

(13) Although more than 5 feet tall is certainly something that
     Socrates and Plato both are, do not suppose that more than
     5 feet tall is something *simpliciter*—that is to say, something
     that can stand independently on its own as substance (Aris-
     totle) or object (Frege).

Infected with solecism, (13) features by way of detachment an
objectionable use of the expression 'more than 5 feet tall' as a
singular term *manqué*, a consideration to which Frege was
actuely sensitive, leading him to insist that what is referred to by a
predicate—for example, 'x is a horse' or 'x is more than 5 feet
tall'—can be referred to only in that manner—that is, predic-
atively. In particular, it can never be referred to by any singular
term, not even by the putative singular term (and this is a famous
paradox): 'what is referred to by the predicative expression "x is
a horse"'. Identified in the first instance as a concept, what the
predicative expression means (refers to, stands for) according to
Frege is finally seen to be a characteristic function, but in either
case the singular terms 'the concept *horse*' and 'the function
horse' fail to refer to any concept or function. Notoriously, Frege
in his paper 'Concept and Object' is prepared to say that 'the
concept *horse* is not a concept' precisely on the ground that 'the
three words "the concept *horse*" do designate an object,'

arguably the set of all horses, 'but on that very account they do not designate a concept'.

Widely regarded as a scandal that is not to be dismissed simply by urging, with Frege, that 'language is here in a predicament', the case is by no means unique. That the average man with his 2.137 children is not a man, one accepts readily enough; and we can even say, drawing on our wayward idiom, that, thanks to his fractional offspring, the average man is something that no human being could possibly be, suggesting that 'the average man' is no more to be construed here as a singular term, despite the presence of the (singular) definite article which Frege takes to be a fairly reliable indicator, than 'the sum of four squares' is to be so regarded in the sentence 'The sum of four squares was proved by Lagrange to be something that every natural number is.' By parity of reasoning, it need not be assumed that 'the concept *horse*' serves as a singular term in the sentence 'The predicate "*x* is a horse" designates the concept *horse*.' Why not rather say that the last three words of the sentence designate this: a horse, but not any particular horse, as in 'A horse is something that Whirlaway and Secretariat both are'. The trouble, of course, is that demonstratives like 'this' and 'that' have long been recognized as singular terms *par excellence*, with at least as much title to being so characterized as proper names like 'Socrates', let alone definite descriptions like 'the present king of France'. So maybe in a certain sort of way—*tropon tina*, as Aristotle would say—Frege's incomplete items can be referred to by singular terms.

If my effort in the previous paragraph, beginning with 'the average man', vindicates Frege only in part, the relevance of the discussion to the whole Aristotelian programme should be evident. For (13) is precisely the sort of statement that Aristotle makes over and over again in his *Metaphysics*, thereby rendering himself vulnerable to the charge of metaphysical solecism. No one doubts, however, that an ungrammatical sentence can be used to express a true proposition; accordingly, the present chapter is to be understood as undertaking—doubtless with only limited success—to express that proposition in some grammatically acceptable form. How Frege can be said to renew and extend the logico-linguistic approach to metaphysics launched by Aristotle,

(13) demonstrates in the most vivid fashion imaginable. Especially salient is the second-order use of 'something', which invites us to exploit the threefold ambiguity of 'is' in an affirmative manner when we propose the ontological slogan 'To be is to be something'. The slogan admits of being glossed in two ways, both of which assign the 'is' of existence to the first occurrence of 'to be'. Regarding the second occurrence of 'to be', on one construal it figures as the 'is' of identity, as complemented with 'something' in its first-order employment. The other construal sees the 'is' of predication as complemented with 'something' in a second-order role, where an instance of being something is being wise or more than 5 feet tall or even self-identical. Elucidating existence twice over, now in terms of identity, now in terms of predication, the slogan is thus to be unpacked in both fashions at once, reminding us of what that master hermeneuticist Humpty-Dumpty called a portmanteau expression.

11

Non-existent Entities

If a centaur is something that neither Socrates nor Plato is, it would appear to be no less the case that a centaur is something that does not exist, and we might accordingly seem forced to concede that in addition to the things that do exist, there are also the things that do not exist, ontology being called upon to accommodate the latter quite as much as the former. In fact, of the two, the non-existing things could only prove the more illuminating, by forcing us to confess that our slogan 'To be is to be something', in so far as it merely undertakes to elucidate existence, has failed even to identify the primary object of metaphysical inquiry, let alone clarify it. Well launched on the way to first principles, we can only relish the opportunity to regress to an ulterior stratum of reality that underlies even existence itself. But no such stratum or substratum, is likely to be found, I believe, though the recent efforts of a new breed of enterprising logicians to rehabilitate Meinong and his gold mountain[1] are all of a piece with the present endeavour to reach the *ne plus ultra* of metaphysics. Success in achieving our goal can be confirmed only by the well-attested failure of efforts to supersede it.

One can certainly think of a gold mountain, urges Meinong, even though no such thing exists, and it must thus be admitted that the gold mountain of which I am thinking has the property of non-existence, just as (presses Anselm) the so-called God of which the atheist is thinking also has that property. But the word 'God' signifies by definition an entity than which nothing greater can be conceived; and it is not to be doubted that any existing entity is greater than any non-existing one. So the atheist turns out to be thinking of something than which something greater *can* be conceived, and he is thus to be convicted of either

[1] See in particular Karel Lambert, *Meinong and the Principle of Independence* (Cambridge: Cambridge University Press, 1983).

contradicting himself or of giving the word 'God' a deviant, non-standard meaning of his own. Meinong's doctrine, widely regarded as a discredited curiosity and dismissed by Ryle in 1972 as one that was 'dead, buried and not going to be resurrected', is now being defended anew by philosophers such as Terence Parsons, who, being logicians first and metaphysicians second, are prepared to carry the logical approach to metaphysics to an extreme from which even I recoil. But one merit must be conceded to them at once. They have an elegant device for blocking the Fregean deduction of Herr Krug's pen, by allowing the first but not the second step of the argument. From the Principle of Identity, they even allow us to deduce that Pegasus is identical with Pegasus, but from that in turn we are not of course allowed to deduce this: $(\exists x)\ x = $ Pegasus. Accordingly, they deny that 'existence' can be glossed as being self-identical, given that Pegasus, even while being self-identical, fails to exist; as a consequence, my whole programme of vindicating ontology in the face of the threefold ambiguity of 'is' is placed very much at risk. Undertaking to meet Meinong half-way in Fregean terms, my own proposal has already been hinted at.

Although it is true that

(1) There are various things that fail to exist—for example, gold mountains and round squares,

it is not the case that

(2) There are non-existing as well as existing things.

But that is perhaps not quite right. For I concede that

(3) A horse is a thing that exists while a centaur is one that does not.

There is thus a second-order reading of (2), on which it comes out as true, but also a first-order reading, the one I initially had in mind, which issues in falsity. Ostensibly framed in a fashion to please Meinong, (1) and (3) can succeed in rendering any genuine Meinongian distinctly uneasy only thanks to the conspicuous absence of the definite article, as in the definite description 'the gold mountain', which Frege and Meinong alike took to be virtually the signature of an object. More even perhaps than the use of the indefinite article in (3), my use of the plural or pseudo-plural in (1) betrays my alienation from Meinongian sympathies. For the second-order plural featured in (1), while allowing us to say that murders have increased in recent years, precludes our asking further (Dummett's test) *which* murders have been increasing in recent years. In portmanteau fashion, conflating a first- and a second-order plural, one may even venture to say, though not without risk of solecism, 'Already this month there have been 36 of those things, namely murders, that have been increasing so alarmingly in recent years.' Here we *can* specify precisely which murders have occurred this month, though it is not of course these murders that have been increasing in recent years. What, then, is it that has been increasing? The number of murders? No, not, at any rate, if 'the number of murders' is taken to be a singular term and one, moreover, that denotes some particular number, for (again) we cannot ask which number it is that has been increasing. That the number of murders has been increasing remains true, of course; it is just that 'the number of murders' can be taken here to be a singular term only if we can find the right sort of thing, which cannot be a number, for it to designate. If it is now urged that one need hardly fret over Frege's insistence that the expression 'the concept *horse*' fails to denote a concept, there is this difference to be noticed. Although there are contexts readily available where 'the number of murders' does denote a number in an altogether unproblematic fashion, Frege will not allow 'the concept *horse*' to denote a concept on any occasion.

When Meinong says, 'The gold mountain is certainly made of gold even though it fails to exist,' I would like to query his definite description by asking, 'Why do you suppose that there is only one non-existent gold mountain?' The whole point of the second-order plural in (1) is to indicate that neither one nor more than one gold mountain is being said to lack existence. More fundamental even than the issue of number—and here I turn from Meinong to Frege—is the question of identity. If one thing that we encounter many times during the day is a cordate—that is, a creature with a heart—then even on those days when no single cordate is encountered by us more than once, is it the case that *another* thing that we encounter exactly as often is a renate—that is, a creature with a kidney? More briefly, speaking again in our wayward idiom, is a cordate something that is identical with a renate? Each cordate is admittedly identical with some renate, and vice versa. The set of cordates is identical with the set of renates, and the genus *cordate*, if the biologist will allow us to speak of such, is doubtless the same as the genus *renate*. Finally, the property of being a cordate is presumably not the same property as that of being a renate. When it comes to the second-order items featured in our wayward idiom, however, I am quite prepared to follow Frege in permitting the whole question of their identity and diversity simply to lapse by default. The predicates 'x is a cordate' and 'x is a renate' being co-extensive, we may then say with Frege that what they designate—namely, characteristic functions—stand to one another in a relation 'analogous' to identity. More radically still, we must acquiesce in the further concession (some will doubtless have to be dragged to this point kicking and screaming) that no Fregean concept or function can be (said to be) so much as identical even with itself (as if there might be something else with which something could be properly identified). So am I conceding, finally, that not everything is identical with itself? By no means.

The upshot of the discussion I take to be that the words 'thing', 'something', and even 'is' undergo a corresponding shift in meaning as we switch back and forth between first- and second-order discourse. The Principle of Identity being asserted in the first-order mode, we need no more qualify it in the face of second-order considerations than an anarchist, on being challenged by riparian considerations, need qualify his assertion that every bank is an outrage against the rights of man. In the one case as in the other the countervailing considerations addressed involve a certifiable equivocation in the use of words. We can even revel in that equivocation by saying, 'Something is something—for example, 5 is odd', where it is not the 'is' of identity that is featured. The word 'something' clearly has a different sense in its second occurrence here from what it has in its first. Objectual in its first occurrence, in its second it might well be termed conceptual or even functional, in keeping with Frege, who turns out now, however, to have been profoundly mistaken in supposing that there are in addition to objects various other items—namely, concepts and functions—as if one were to undertake to say in portmanteau fashion, 'Socrates is one thing, 5 is another, and a third is something that Socrates is, namely wise.'

That there really is a fourth sense of 'is' in addition to the standard three, the juxtaposition of (4), (5), and (6) strongly suggests.

(4)   Wise is one thing that Socrates is, in Athens another, while a man is a third such thing that Socrates is.

(5)   Socrates is wise, in Athens and a man.

(6)   Socrates has the property of being wise, the property of being in Athens, and the property of being a man.

(7)   Socrates is a member of the set of wise things, the set of things in Athens, and the set of men.

Although largely supernumerary here, (7) has been tossed in because it is not only (4), (5), and (6), but (7) as well, that may be taken in a bundle to 'say the same thing' in some rough-and-ready fashion. (5) is worth lingering over for its own sake, in connection with Aristotle. Smacking of zeugma, the sentence 'Socrates is (both) wise and in Athens' strikes one as less than fully grammatical, thereby providing some support for Aristotle's thesis that the 'is' of predication is itself equivocal on its own whenever different categories are involved, as in the present case where those of quality and place are featured. Inflated beyond any immediate need, (4), (5), and (6) illustrate the central issue regarding the ontology of predication: namely, the famous problem of universals, which may be trimmed down to basics as follows:

(8)   Socrates is wise.

(9)   There is something that Socrates is, namely wise.

(10)   Socrates has wisdom (has the property of being wise).

Repositioned, the second-order sentence has been contrived to serve as a *tertium quid* intermediate between the less problematic

(8) and (10). If the first occurrence of 'is' in (9) strikes one as being the 'is' of existence, one is hard pressed to state exactly what it is that is being said to exist. The easy answer is to gloss (9) as saying that there exists a certain property—namely, wisdom—that belongs to Socrates, and that in fact accords precisely with the routine, non-Fregean hermeneutics (= semantics) of second-order logic. Because any such assimilation of (9) to (10) can be readily resisted as inflationary, one may choose rather to have (9) collapse back into (8), whereupon the problematic 'is' proves to be the 'is' of predication, albeit disguised as that of existence. This 'minimalist', reductive gloss results in (9) being taken as a 'puffed up' version of (8). If in a non-committal vein one may speak of the second-order sense of 'is' in (9), whatever it might turn out to be, it is evident that clarity regarding it presupposes an antecedent clarity concerning (8) and (10), which are themselves by no means as unproblematic as one might be forgiven for supposing.

Above all, there is the logical question of whether (8) entails (10). Is the argument '(8), therefore (10)' to be certified as valid? Which is as much as to ask whether in every possible world where (8) is true (10) is true as well. And here the obvious answer is yes, if only because (8) and (10) appear to be saying the same thing, albeit using somewhat different words. Admittedly, there is at least a difference in 'tone' between (8) and (10), as (10) can be seen to be a dressed-up version of (8), and (8) in its turn as a shirt-sleeve version of (10). Even granting now that (8) and (10) do have the same meaning for all practical purposes, the philosopher must insist on there being a profound difference between them on the level of metaphysical grammar. The metaphysical difference is closely related to a manifest difference in logical form. For if (8), on the strength of the monadic predicate 'x is wise' exhibits the logical form 'Fa'—that is, 'a is (an) F', (10) instantiates the form 'aRb'—that is, a is related to b, thanks to its dyadic predicate 'x has y.' Assenting to (10) thus commits us, if only nominally, to the existence of two things, Socrates and wisdom, whereas subscribing to (8) commits us, overtly, at least, only to one. 'Speaking for myself,' says the nominalist, 'when I am found asserting (10), I am to be taken as being only nominally committed to the existence of wisdom'; and that, as Humpty-Dumpty explained to Alice, explains precisely why it is that ever since the Middle Ages the anti-Platonist has been called a nominalist.

If the transformation of (8) into (10) is in fact described grammatically as involving a process of nominalization whereby the (concrete) general term 'wise', which is an adjective, yields the (abstract) singular term 'wisdom', which is a noun, the process is specified more metaphysically, and often pejoratively, by another word: 'reification', which is as much as to say 'thingification', or even (by way of express contrast with the nominalist) Platonization. This process—call it nominalization or reification as you please—whereby 'wise' in (8) is transformed into 'wisdom' in (10) can now be seen as proceeding *through* (9), though arresting the process at (9) yields only a quasi-thing, 'wise' retaining its adjectival form, at any rate if 'thing' is used in its primary, not its secondary, sense. As the theory of what it is to be a thing (anything), ontology is concerned above all with things in the primary sense of the word; but it is also concerned secondarily and in *pros hen* fashion with the many things that Socrates is, as well as the many things that he is not. But that is not quite to say, 'Some of the things with which ontology is concerned are first-order in character, while others are merely second-order.' What sense does the word 'things' have here? 'Thing' is admittedly a factotum sort of word with a 'roving commission' of its own that affords it a flexibility adaptive to almost any context; in any case, if the word 'bank' can after all be assigned a third sense disjunctively encompassing the other two, why not a corresponding innovation with the word 'thing'? If banks$_1$ and banks$_2$ can both be banks$_3$, why can't things$_1$ and things$_2$ both be things$_3$? In effect, one is being asked to rescue the following 'sentence' from solecism. Wise being one of the things that Socrates is, wise must be one of the things$_3$ with which ontology is concerned. It is not, however, the word 'thing' or 'thing$_3$' that causes trouble here, but the word 'wise' in its second occurrence. Cooking up a third sense of 'thing' will be otiose unless it can succeed somehow in imposing on 'wise' the sense of 'wisdom'; indeed, the Platonist argues that since wise is one of the things that Socrates is, any investigation of that thing can only be an inquiry into the nature of wisdom, thereby shifting in Frege's terms from a concept to an object. Oddly enough, however, Frege's concepts and functions are themselves to be counted as at least quasi-platonic entities, however deficient they might appear in their incompleteness.

Although this issue of Platonism emerges as the central question in the theory of predication, it has only surfaced properly in the present chapter. Content in the previous one merely to provide the larger framework within which the issue might be posed, we here employ it as the battleground of nominalist versus Platonist. Because the nominalist is inclined to regard the transformation of concrete general terms into abstract singular ones as consisting of scarcely more than the merest turn or even trick of language, reification will be seen by him to be just another rhetorical trope, along with metaphor, hyperbole, personification, zeugma, and so forth, all of which are systematically studied by the poetics of ordinary, as well as elevated, discourse. Precisely by recognizing the trope of reification as a trick of language, the nominalist is in effect taking (10) to be true only on a non-literal reading, thereby conceding that the literal meaning of (10) cannot be identical with that of (8). There is an evident difficulty here. Metaphysics aside, (8) and (10) being pragmatically interchangeable with one another in virtually every context, one can hardly deny that they have the same meaning. Glossed in terms of Quine's logico-ontological hermeneutics, however, by differing in their (at any rate explicit) ontological commitments they must be allowed *a fortiori* to differ in meaning as well.

Faced with this paradox it is no wonder that Quine should despair of the notion of meaning, in particular sameness of meaning, as scientifically reputable; and it is here that his maxim 'No entity without identity' comes directly into play. In asking if the meaning of (8) is identical with that of (10), we are invoking the abstract singular term 'the meaning of (8)', which ostensibly picks out an item that is or is not identical with what 'the meaning of (10)' designates. Concluding ruefully that there may be 'no fact of the matter' here available even to God in his omniscience, one may feel with Quine that the identity conditions associated with our informal notion of meaning are simply too vague or ambiguous to stand up to the kind of punishment that serious research cannot fail to administer. Meanings will then drop out of one's ontology, though they may be replaced by other entities that are designed to be in this or that respect functionally equivalent to them, as when we say that, waiving the question of meaning as such, (8) and (10) have the same pragmatic, but different ontological, import. Or when in answer to the question of whether 'the Morning Star' and 'the Evening Star' mean the same thing, we reply with Frege, yes and no. Yes, they do mean the same thing in so far as they denote the same object—namely, the planet Venus. No, they do not mean the same thing in so far as they differ in sense—that is, express different concepts. Sense and reference thus replace the omnibus notion of meaning. We have there in fact a thumb-nail sketch of what goes on in the ontology of theory building when one sort of entity comes to be superseded by others, for, as Quine's slogan has it, explication is elimination. My own suggestion that Meinong's non-existent entities be accommodated under the heading of second-order things can be seen to be a still more devious case of supersession. For Pegasus is finally seen to be something with which nothing can properly be said to be identical, not even Pegasus.

Part III

12

Quinean Poetics

If poetics in the broad sense of the term is the study of the non-literal, as opposed to the literal, use of language, where the very contrast between the two is decisive, the nominalist's refusal to construe abstract singular terms at face value, as at least undertaking (whether successfully or not) to refer to trans-empirical entities, can only be regarded as an audacious exercise in poetics. The Platonist now turns out to be the merest literalist, and despite his searching critique of the poets, Plato is liable to the charge of having himself been duped by a figure of speech, albeit the most profound of all, the trope of reification.

If the simplest sort of case is provided by (10) in the previous chapter, which featured wisdom as well as Socrates, a more complex example is found here in (2).

(1) There are exactly as many apples in this basket as there are plums in that one.
(2) The number of apples in this basket is exactly the same as the number of plums in that one.

On the face of it (2) might appear to be merely making explicit what (1) is content to take for granted: namely, the existence of numbers. How (1) can be glossed so as to purge it of any implicit reference to numbers, Frege in effect explained when he provided us with a recipe for translating into the canonical notation of first-order predicate logic every adjectival use of number-words, along the lines of (4) in Chapter 6. Appealing to that recipe, the nominalist can explicate his semantics for (1) as follows. Any sentence of the form 'There are exactly as many F's as G's' will be true if and only if some sentence of the form 'There are exactly n F's and there are exactly n G's' is antecedently true, where n features the adjectival use of some number-word. Thanks then to the fact that (4) in Chapter 6 exempts us from any commitment to numbers, (1) proves to be at a remove equally exonerated. It is now open to one to insist that, after allowing for the rhetorical trope of reification, (2) is reducible to (1).

Philosophy aside, what *do* we mean when we utter sentences like (2) in everyday life? Although Quine fights shy of appeals to introspection in answering such questions, his stress on behaviouristic considerations is the merest distraction. By all means use introspection. In uttering (2), is one committing oneself only to the existence of apples and plums (and baskets), as in the case of (1), or is there a further commitment to numbers, let it be only for the nonce? Most readers consulting their own introspective experience will find great difficulty in answering my question, and we may thus score one point against Cartesian introspective mentalism for future reference. It is easy enough, however, to imagine an English-speaking society in which everyone is genetically programmed to be an instinctive Platonist (or nominalist). In such a society my query would be answered like a pistol shot, and any hesitation might well be regarded as conceptually impossible. Surely one must know what one means when one says something! If in our own society there is a strong predisposition to nominalism, still one hesitates, if only because it seems extraordinary to suppose that typical utterances of (2) are meant non-literally. Quite apart from the Cartesian issue, one does suppose that there can be no great mystery as to whether a certain expression, used indiffferently by oneself or others, is meant literally; and yet the spectre of 'indeterminacy in radical translation' comes home to roost vividly enough even in regard to intra-English or English–English translation when the nominalist proposes (1) as an adequate paraphrase of (the purely cognitive content) of (2) in its pragmatic use. I think we should allow that in this or that man's idiolect, (2) should be glossed literally—that is, Platonistically—or non-literally—that is, nominalistically—as the case may be, even while we concede to Quine that in the standard case there is an ineradicable indeterminacy or ambiguity between the two readings of (2). Poetry and ontology alike may thus be seen to be incipiently emerging in the ambiguous role played by the abstract singular term of our mother tongue, though one is surprised to find that it is the down-to-earth nominalist and not the visionary Platonist whose ear is peculiarly sensitive to the 'poetry' of (2). In fact, it is Quine who has trained us to hear the music of ontological commitment in all sorts of discourse, scientific and vulgar alike.

Poetry in the literal sense of the word is not far from my mind. Alerted by Quine, one need look no further than the first line of the foundational poem of the West, where 'the anger of Achilles' is featured as transformationally generated by nominalization from the basic sentence 'Achilles is angry.' Poetically enough, then, the *Iliad* is expressly launched with the reification of its hero's anger, which will be manifested in fourfold fashion in the course of the poem, preliminarily against Agamemnon, then generalized to all the Greeks, and later, after being addressed climactically to Hector, extended in turn towards all the Trojans. Having earlier, in Chapter 7, had occasion to distinguish between ontological and rhetorical tropes, we are free to say in a neutral vein that glossing the first line of the poem consists above all in recognizing the trope of reification. One leaves open, at least initially, the possibility that the poet intends the trope literally and ontologically rather than non-literally and 'poetically', tropes in general being taken etymologically as any turn of language—for example, any passive transformation of the active voice. If it should seem obvious that Homer as poet must surely be taken as issuing his trope in the 'poetic' mode, I can only recommend thinking again. Although poetry does consist principally of the non-literal, against that background the card of truth can always be played straight. Suppose that the anger of Achilles is being hypostasized as an elemental force in its own right that the 'goddess' is being urged to 'sing', for she is not being asked merely to sing *about* that anger. Played as straight ontology, rather than mere 'poetry', Homer's trope may well come richly into its own simply as poetry. If I were merely urging that Homer be taken as a Platonist *avant la lettre*, my suggestion might be readily dismissed. It is to be noticed, however, that 'the anger of Achilles', while grammatically identifiable as an abstract singular term, cannot possibly be glossed as referring to any Platonic entity properly so-called. No one could suppose the anger of Achilles to be identical with the anger of (say) Henry V at

Harfleur, though the shape of this cup one presumes to be identical with the shape of that one (they belong to the same kitchen set), and the property of being angry doubtless belongs to the two heroes. How very particular Achilles' anger is, the first line indicates when one transcribes it word for word in the fashion of a school crib. 'The anger sing, O goddess, of the son of Peleus, Achilles.' It is almost as if it were an essential property of this very anger that it belongs to Achilles, who in turn is seen perhaps as having as one of his essential properties being a son of the man Peleus.

If the first of the two suggestions, that this particular anger could not possibly 'inhere' in anyone but Achilles, invites us to recall Aristotle, the appeal to essence in the second one can be associated with Aristotle only indirectly, thanks to the recent work of Saul Kripke and his 'necessities of origin'. In Aristotle one does find explicitly entertained—and even (in the *Categories*) endorsed—the notion that the whiteness of this wall is distinct from the whiteness of that one, even if the two walls are (as we say) the exact same shade of white. With localized items of this sort, commonly styled as abstract particulars or quality-instances, the nominalist *qua* nominalist need have no very serious misgivings, and we can thus distinguish soft from hard nominalism. While the hard nominalist denies outright that abstract singular terms refer to anything whatever, the soft nominalist takes them to denote such localized quality-instances as the anger of Achilles.

Hard and soft Platonism may be correspondingly contrasted as follows. While the soft Platonist posits merely a certain universal whiteness that is present in all white things but which could not possibly exist in the absence of any concrete entity's actually being white, the hard Platonist subscribes to the existence outside all space and time of a transcendent abstract entity, whiteness, that is in no way parasitic on there being any concrete things that are white. Although this ultra-Platonism has usually been regarded as an extravagant doctrine, ever since it was subjected to Aristotle's critique, which objected principally to the *separation* between each thing and its attributes, it is only in taking the long historical view that matters appear in that light. Closer to home and largely under the sponsorship of Frege and Quine, hard Platonism has often come to appear scarcely more than the merest common sense, and an unreconstructed nominalist like Nelson Goodman could for two decades be widely regarded by professional philosophers as positively Neanderthal. Again, the issue can be seen to be at least in the first instance a question in straight logic.

(3) Nothing is white.
(4) Nothing has the property of being white.
(5) There is something that is (identical with) the property of being white.

Taken informally and at face value, the argument '(3) therefore (4) therefore (5)' certainly appears to be valid. In any possible world where (3) is true, (4) and (5) would appear to be true as well. But then (5) must surely be true in every possible world whatever, let white things be present or absent. If (3) is then a contingent falsehood, (5) must be a necessary truth, and hard Platonism is vindicated.

However one decides on the purely logical issue (and one will wish to consider as well the argument '(1) therefore (2)'), when it comes to the poetics of the *Iliad* it is soft nominalism that is directly relevant; and, recalling William Empson with his seven types of ambiguity, we should probably rejoice in the ambiguity of 'the anger . . . of Achilles' as to whether it is to be taken as involving an ontological or a rhetorical trope. There is this further consideration. Granted that the *Iliad* features two Achillean anger-instances above all, targeted on Agamemnon and Hector, in addition to lesser ones, why suppose that the definite description 'the anger . . . of Achilles' succeeds in referring to anything whatever? Platonist and nominalist alike are entitled to insist on a failure of reference here, one that is redeemed, however, by being a plus for the poetry. In the Platonizing spirit of one over many, the poet may be viewed as postulating as a 'theoretical entity' a unitary anger-instance, *the* anger of Achilles, in order to account for the many Achillean anger-instances; and it will then be that theoretical entity that the goddess is called upon to sing. Absurd? Even a contradiction in terms, this conceit of mine—singing a theoretical entity? Well, it does encroach upon deep stereotypes that govern modern thought, principally the opposition of science and poetry, though one might suppose it to be precisely the task of philosophy to query such stereotypes.

Realistically speaking, why not take 'the anger of Achilles' to refer unitarily to a certain character trait—namely, the irascibility of our hero? Ah, yes, that is indeed realism with a vengeance, as when we speak of the realism of the nineteenth-century novel. If singing a character trait *is* absurd, the suggestion still needs to be taken seriously on its own ground. At ease principally with the lyric poem and the novel, we are prone to find the *Iliad* falling disconcertingly betwixt and between the one and the other, and we are thus motivated to find a way of cherishing the ambiguity. Read as a novel in the mode of prose, the poem does involve the reification of a character trait, for it is not to be supposed that 'the irascibility of Achilles', itself an abstract singular term, refers to some unproblematic empirical matter of fact that lies entirely open to observation. Irascibility being dispositional in character (in line with the Ryle of Chapter 7), it will lead us into the whole issue of counterfactuals and the metaphysics of possible worlds; accordingly, I can only salute the efforts of the French school to 'deconstruct' the positivistic photo-realism of the nineteenth-century novel. Transformationally derived by way of Latinization, as well as nominalization, from the basic sentence 'Achilles is quick to anger', the 'irascibility of Achilles', while signifying something of the deepest metaphysical import, takes us in the direction of prose rather than poetry. Postulating now more or less literally some single actualization of that disposition, the poem can be taken lyrically as the singing of an elemental force to which the *furor poeticus* of the poet himself (as it will later come to be called) can be seen to answer; accordingly, one finds the following conceit in Edmund Spenser. There being a certain 'mighty rage' with which the 'sacred Muse' can be found to 'infest' the 'hearts of great heroes', it proves to be identical with the 'furious fit' that the Muse instils into the 'feeble breast' of the poet himself when he undertakes to 'sing . . . of wars and bloody Mars'.[1]

Poetic and ontological at the same time, reification proceeds

---

[1] Spenser, *Faerie Queene*, I. xi. 5–7.

here in one-over-many fashion to postulate an unexpected universal that is instantiated in poet and hero alike. One understands now how it can be that on the moral level Homer, as a reasonable man, can only deplore the truculence of his hero, even while on an aesthetic plane he cannot but feel himself closely attuned to it. The affinity may be more than merely aesthetic. More or less in earnest, Plato glosses a line in Homer featuring Ocean as a case where, in effect, the poet, viewed broadly as a materialist and a relativist, 'has said that all things are the offspring of flow and motion',[2] proving thus to be indeed a Heraclitean *avant la lettre*. By way of expressing a dyadic relation, the predicate 'x is an offspring of y' requires a semantics whereby the predicate is 'satisfied' by various ordered pairs of entities—for example < Achilles, Peleus > . The second slot is the hard one to fill on the cosmic level, for even if one were to construe 'flow' and 'motion' as singular terms referring to some property (or property-instance or universal), say the property of undergoing incessant change, that seems too abstract an entity to fill the bill. Far from being merely metaphorical (the joke is on Plato if he thought so), Ocean is exactly suited for the job, and we can even say that by invoking it, the poet succeeds in reifying change, if not indeed chaos, as a concrete, efficacious entity. It turns out now that by proximately singing the anger of Achilles, who is the offspring of a sea-nymph, the poet may well be giving voice to the ultimate principle of reality itself, whose representation circumscribes the uttermost rim of Achilles' shield.

If the failure of the classical rhetoricians to identify the trope of reification in the first line of the *Iliad* leads to Virgil's being content to sing arms and the man (the trace of zeugma here is not without interest of its own), there has been the more general failure to recognize how deeply poetry and ontology connect with one another, to their mutual enrichment. For reification is precisely what ontology is all about, as one or another theoretical entity, everything being such according to Quine, is postulated by us in threefold fashion as an object (1) to which we refer, (2) of which we predicate, and (3) over which we quantify; and it may be proposed that a Quinean poetics must be what Wallace

---

[2] Plato, *Theaetetus*, 152e.

Stevens was gesturing towards when he wrote, 'There probably is available in reality something accessible through a theory of poetry which would make a profound difference in our sense of the world.'

13

Sets

If we want to say that Socrates is wise, one roundabout way of saying it is this:

(1) $(\exists x)$ Socrates $\epsilon\ x\ \cdot\ x\ =\ \hat{y}\ (y$ is wise).

That is to say, there exists an x such that both Socrates is a member of it and it is identical with the set of all y's such that y is wise. It is the ϵ of set-membership to which I particularly wish to draw attention, since the mathematician Peano introduced it by way of express allusion to the Greek word *esti*, meaning 'is'. The 'is' of predication is thus to be elucidated logically, if not ontologically, in terms of the dyadic relation 'x is a member of y'—that is, $x\ \epsilon\ y$, which can be seen to be the mathematical counterpart of the relation 'x has (as one of its properties) y'. Set theory thus offers the promise of a complete mathematization of the 'is' of predication. Of the three senses of 'is', it is the predicative sense that emerged for us as primary, for one has only to consult the schema 'to be is to be F' to see at a glance that the 'is' of existence is being elucidated by (and accordingly reduced to) that of predication. Suppose now that the specific predicate 'x is self-identical' is chosen to fill the slot in the schema. Then the 'is' of predication takes precedence over the 'is' of identity as well, at least in the sense that being self-identical is a particular instance of being F. The primacy of predicative being having been assured, set theory now emerges as the mathematics of being as such, or being *qua* being. That logic is just set theory can come to seem perfectly obvious if one considers how perspicuously the traditional syllogism can be represented in it. 'All men are mortal' is glossed (or paraphrased) as 'The set of men is included in the set of mortals'—that is, $h \subset m$. And after 'All Greeks are men' is represented by '$g \subset h$', the conclusion '$g \subset m$' drops out at once. Defining this new piece of notation '$x \subset y$'

expressing *set inclusion* is easy enough, for it is merely an abbreviated way of saying this: (z) $z \in x \supset z \in y$. Set inclusion is thus
sharply distinguished from set membership, as the set of Greeks
is found to be included in, but not a member of, the set of men.

Notice above all my use of the words 'gloss' and 'paraphrase'.
For if in the previous chapter (2) was glossed ontologically *down-
wards* as (1), here 'All men are mortal' is being glossed upwards
into set theory, seeing that in the one case a certain sort of
entity—namely, numbers—was expressly eliminated, while in the
present one a new object has been ostentatiously introduced: so
ostentatiously in fact that until Quine blew the whistle, philosophers were characteristically oblivious to how much metaphysics they were buying into when they yielded to the invitation
to eke out their logical lexicon, consisting of x, $\sim$, $\cdot$, $\supset$, $(\exists x)$,
(x) and $=$, with this interloper $\in$. That in tendentiously identifying
logic with set theory we are already up to our necks, if not positively over our heads, awash in metaphysics, Quine has decisively
established, and it is surprising only that something so obvious
should have taken so long to recognize. Against the background
of Kant, Frege and his contemporaries ought surely to have been
struck by the way in which the so-called pure sets above all—that
is, the empty set, the set whose only member is the empty set, the
set with the previous two sets as its only members, and so on—
qualify as noumena. Even today most Kant scholars will doubtless shudder at my suggestion that the term 'noumenon' might be
applied with propriety to pure sets, if not to sets in general. That
the Kantian distinction between phenomena (things that appear
to sense perception) and noumena (objects of pure thought or
intellection) has its provenance in Plato, no one doubts; and
thanks to Plato's expressly using the word *noumena* to characterize his Forms by way of contrast with *phenomena*, it is very much
in keeping with the Platonic lexicon that pure sets should so
qualify as well. Objects of pure reason that are inaccessible to
sense perception, pure sets could not but be regarded by Kant as
precisely the sort of super-sensible entity that his *Critique of Pure
Reason* was designed to deconstruct. How then anticipate that
they would surface in the austere science of logic itself? Doubtless it is the very austerity of logic, enhanced indeed by its

intimidating renewal in mathematical guise, that diverted attention away from the possibility of contraband goods being smuggled into it, no less than an infinite supply of noumena in the specific form of pure sets.

One is free of course to bandy with pure sets, not to mention sets in general, in the guise of a *façon de parler*, and on this antiseptic view sentences featuring pure sets are to be glossed non-literally by the hermeneutics supplied by our ontological poetics. How the rhetorical trope of reification comes specifically into play here, the following sentence helps to explain: 'The absence of centaurs from the continent of Europe had long been remarked on in the taxonomies of the biologists.' A singular term on the face of it, 'the absence of centaurs' positively invites us to engage in reification by positing the set of all centaurs, or all centaurs in Europe, as its semantic correlative. With the mathematician Dedekind one can go so far as to argue that the very notion of an empty set is a contradiction in terms, on the ground that a set is constituted by its members. No members, no set. The convenience afforded by the empty set Dedekind readily conceded, for the mathematician cannot but wish to prove theorems concerning the set of all counter-examples to Goldbach's conjecture, that every even number is the sum of two prime numbers, even though no one at present knows whether there are any. Systematic considerations alone are thus seen to pressure us into operating with the empty set willy-nilly, and one is not surprised that Frege, who could not possibly be satisfied with Dedekind's anti-realist solution—namely, to conjure with the empty set as a convenient fiction—should propose a realist one of his own. A set is rather to be defined as the extension of a predicate (or concept or function), and as the logicians of Frege's time had no hesitation when it came to invoking the extension of 'x is (an) F' across the board, which one informally defines as 'all the things which are F', an empty set ceases to be an anomaly. Even a zero extension was allowed to be an extension. As a proof of the empty set, Frege's line of argument is undermined by one consideration above all. Drawing on the wisdom of hindsight, there is the embarrassing predicate 'x is not a member of x' (call it the Russell predicate) that was shown by Bertrand Russell to have no extension whatever, not even the empty set, assuming of course that the extension of a predicate must be a set if it is anything at all. So one cannot posit an empty set simply on the ground that every predicate determines a set. Many things do satisfy the Russell predicate—for example, Julius Caesar, if only because it is not to be supposed that he is any sort of set at all, and one can even quantify over 'all the things that are F' in the case at hand. Even so, there cannot possibly be a set encompassing just those things, as a contradiction can be derived from the supposition. Assume there to be a set, R, of everything that is not a member of itself. Well, is R a member of R? If it is, then (by definition of R) it is not a member of R. So R cannot be a member of R. But then R qualifies as a member of R by satisfying the Russell predicate.

Although 'the extension of the predicate "x is (an) F" ' is informally explained by way of 'all the things that are F', there proves to be a decisive difference between the two expressions, as the one, but not the other, figures grammatically as a singular term, and it is precisely this gathering up of a 'many' into a 'one' that takes us into the essence of sets, numbers, and concepts. Always a bit skittish about sets, Frege never ceased to emphasize their secondary role as compared with concepts (and functions). In fact, by defining a set as the extension of a concept, the primacy of the concept was assured. After Russell, however, Frege's approach to sets was widely felt to be unacceptable, and there was to be much wandering in the set-theoretical wilderness before the promised land was sighted, in the form of the so-called ZF intuition into the nature of sets, discussion of which is deferred to a later chapter.

If one motive for preferring impure sets to pure ones lies in the fact that the former commit us merely to soft Platonism, while the latter requires the hard variety, impure sets merit attention in their own right. As to mere first-level sets, like the set of books or the set of chairs in this room, doubt has been expressed as to whether they should be classified as theoretical (= noumenal) rather than observational (= phenomenal) entities. A set theory that allows only first-level sets is scarcely deserving of the name, and it is only with the recognition of second-level sets—for example, the set K_3 whose only two members are the two previously mentioned first-level sets, K_1 and K_2—that set theory properly comes into its own; and even here there is a further refinement that must be respected. The set K_4 that has as a member each chair and each book in this room must not be confused with K_3. Anyone who suspects that K_3 and K_4 may really be one and the same, even though the proper names 'K_3' and 'K_4' were introduced through somewhat different descriptions, must be taking those proper names to be denoting something other than sets in the mathematical sense of the term 'set'. Any such suspicion can arise only out of failure to notice that K_3 was defined as having precisely two members, whereas K_4 (and here I am admittedly imparting fresh information) has exactly forty-six. We can now complete the argument by appealing directly to Leibniz's law:

$$(1)\ (x)\,(y)\,(\exists F)\, Fx \cdot \sim\! Fy \supset \sim\!(x = y).$$

Resorting to our wayward idiom, we are saying here that for every x and every y, if there is something that x is which y is not, then x and y are not identical. Well, one thing that K_4 is and that K_3 is not is a set whose members are all non-sets—namely, books and chairs. Although K_1 and K_2 are not members of K_4, they are indeed included in it. Pursuaded that the basic content of K_3 is the same as that of K_4, one may feel with Nelson Goodman that the various points of difference between K_3 and K_4 are simply too 'precious', too noumenal, too metaphysical even, to be taken with ontological seriousness. Nominally different, K_3 and K_4 may be seen to the same in reality, and what that reality consists in one may choose to elucidate through mereology, which has been described as the poor man's set theory, as devised by Polish logicians. In any event, sets can hardly be elucidated except by way of contrast with their counterparts in mereology, which undertakes to axiomatize an extended 'logic' of the part–whole relation.

One is asked to believe initially that there is a certain scattered object (Hawaii and Alaska being parts of it) that is the USA. Consider now that scattered whole, W_1, that may be somewhat metaphorically said to the 'fusion' of all the states of the USA. Consider (also) the scattered whole, W_2, that is the 'fusion' of all the counties of the USA. Then W_1 is indeed identical with W_2, though when it comes to 'dissecting' the USA into (perhaps non-overlapping) parts, there are various ways of going about the job, two of which have been indicated. Set theory, by contrast, insists that the set of states is emphatically a different entity from the set of counties; and while the 'fusion' or mereological 'sum' of this page and France is a scattered whole that can be variously decomposed into two or more parts, the corresponding set must be allowed to have exactly two members, absolutely speaking. Set theory being characteristically committed to the Pairing Axiom

$$(2)\quad (x)\,(y)\,(\exists z)\, x \in z \cdot y \in z,$$

mereology takes the following 'axiom' to be foundational:

$$(3)\quad (x)\,(y)\,(\exists z)\, x \text{ is a 'part' of } z \cdot y \text{ is a 'part' of } z.$$

My use of scare quotes here is merely designed to help one query whether the mereologist is using the words 'part' and 'whole' in their literal senses.

This whole question of literal and non-literal, having emerged for us as thematic in the previous chapter, invites us, more generally, to project what one can only call the poetics of the sciences, taken to be a study of those items featured in the Book of Science that are to be glossed non-literally. As our bible, the Book of Science is presumed to contain only true sentences, but it is less clear how they are to be construed, which literally and which non-literally, and it is thus to be expected that almost as much acrimonious dispute will arise in the field of scientific, as in that of biblical, hermeneutics. Continuing along this line, a further issue is inescapable. At least since Aristotle, mainstream philosophy has been characteristically committed to what we might call the literalist thesis: namely, that anything worth saying, at least in science and philosophy, be it true or false, can be expressed without recourse to the non-literal, though it is not to be doubted that in practice metaphors and the like serve to cut short what would otherwise extend into tedious stretches of mindless exposition (metaphors as expediters). Taken as a point of principle, however, the literalist thesis can even be said to be constitutive of main-line philosophy, and whenever a thinker—Heidegger comes notably to mind—ostentatiously transgresses that principle, he is taken at once to be opting out of main-line philosophy.

Because my encounter with poetry in the previous chapter might be felt to undermine my standing as a card-carrying professional philosopher, it might be supposed that I would hesitate to subscribe to the literalist thesis. Not so. Never has one of my more profound thoughts struck me as in any way resisting articulation in purely literal terms. But that is a minority report of one, and though it can hardly fail to carry weight with me, my readers can only be expected to acknowledge it in passing, as meagre evidence in support of the literalist thesis. As to evidence *against* the thesis, there is one item above all that stands out from the entire history of philosophy, the following passage from Frege's 'Concept and Object':

> It must indeed be recognized that here we are confronted by an awkwardness of language, which I admit cannot be avoided, if we say that the concept *horse* is not a concept whereas, e.g., the city of Berlin is a city and the volcano Vesuvius is a volcano. Language is here in a predicament that justifies the departure from custom.[1]

A mere 'awkwardness of language', forsooth, when it is no less than a 'predicament' that 'cannot be avoided'! As to 'the departure from custom' that Frege's deviant use of language involves, it may be said to smack of catachresis in the etymological sense of the term, though more specifically it turns out that nothing less than the language of outright contradiction—Empson's seventh type of ambiguity—is being pressed into service as the vehicle of a true proposition. It is 'by a kind of necessity of language', writes Frege, that 'my expressions taken literally sometimes miss my thought; I mention an object when what I intend is a concept.' Drawing heavily on our wayward idiom, an effort to state in purely literal terms what Frege is after might go as follows:

> 'Although a horse is one of the many things that Socrates is not, that thing is not something that can be referred to by a singular term, all such being objects, though it is indeed referred to (albeit in a predicative or conceptual fashion) when we say that it is not the case that Socrates is a horse.'

[1] G. Frege, *Collected Papers on Mathematics, Logic and Philosophy*, ed. B. McGuinness (Oxford: Blackwell, 1984), pp. 185–6.

The trouble of course is that both the expression 'that thing' in the second clause and the pronoun 'it' in the third clause can only be construed grammatically as singular terms which do (undertake to) refer to the very thing that the sentence insists cannot be referred to by any such expression.

Eking out the literal, Frege now resorts expressly to the trope of metaphor when he says that, by contrast with objects, concepts—that is, characteristic functions—are unsaturated or incomplete, where it is not only 'unsaturated' that is being used metaphorically but 'incomplete' as well. Taking the metaphor with full serious-ness—I almost said 'literally'—I am tempted to argue as follows. Just as a half-built house, being radically incomplete, is not a house, so an incomplete entity is not an entity, since, like 'counter-feit' and 'dead', 'half-built' and 'incomplete' are to be classified as what medieval logicians called *alienans* terms. Virtually anticipating my objection, Frege says that, while incomplete on their own, concepts and functions are completed when they fea-ture in thoughts—that is, mind-independent propositions; and it may be that a deeper understanding of Frege, beyond any I have succeeded in achieving, will vindicate his conviction that 'founded deep in the nature of things' are items that are truly incomplete in the sense that they fail to satisfy all the conditions that are required if something is to be an object (of reference, predication, and quantification), where two conditions in particular are men-tioned: (*a*) being susceptible of reference (by a singular term) and (*b*) being identical with or distinct from anything whatever. In the meantime, pending further enlightenment, I can only follow Quine and insist non-trivially that everything—well, everything in the primary sense of the word 'thing'—is an object. As to the truth value of the literalist thesis, the poetics of philosophy must con-tinue to insist that Frege provides us with the *experimentum crucis* to decide the issue, even while relishing the irony that the issue comes to a head not in connection with the more romantic sorts of philosophy, but with the very foundations of the analytical school itself.

14

Numbers

'Mathematics has come to be identical with philosophy for modern thinkers,' Aristotle surprises us by writing in the first book of the *Metaphysics*, at 992a.33, referring to the aggressive Platonists of his day, whom he takes to have joined forces with a renewed Pythagoreanism. If the sense of *déjà vu* is inescapable, it is set theory above all that provides the link. Mathematics being widely thought to be reducible to set theory, set theory in its turn has been seen to connect on the deepest level with both logic and ontology, through the theory of predication. There is a further consideration to be noticed. Grounded in the theory of predication, metaphysics is held by Aristotle and Kant alike to culminate in a theory of the super-sensible, and the super-sensible flourishes nowhere more luxuriantly than in the noumenal entities, impure as well as pure, of set theory. Finally, and with specific reference to the ostensible primacy of physics when it comes to any authoritative account of reality, pure mathematics is recognized as providing the underlying framework of the science, in the form of the extended number system. Meta-physics is thus the theory of that system which, as constituted by the natural numbers, reaches out to include negative, rational, irrational, and imaginary numbers as well.

The rudiments of the theory will be recalled from Chapter 6, where the notation of predicate logic *sans* set theory (and *a fortiori sans* mathematics) was seen to suffice when it comes to discharging the role of the (natural) number-words in their adjectival use. If their substantial use was found to be more challenging, even there resources are available for producing valid statement forms of predicate logic that succeed fairly well in mimicking such arithmetic truths as that $5 + 7 = 12$, which on the face of it commit us to the existence of numbers. We can pretend, however, that the equation says something like this: there are exactly 5 *F*'s and there are exactly 7 *G*'s ⊃ there are at least 12 *H*'s, where the numerals figure only as adjectives. Of course, we shall have to add the following restrictions: (a) (*x*) *Fx* ⊃ ~ *Gx* and (b) (*x*) (*Fx* x *Gx*) ⊃ *Hx*. Even so, only a rough gloss on the equation has been given. Precisely as an *equation*, it is not enough to construe '5 + 7 = 12' as a one-way street of the form '*p* · *q* ⊃ *r*'. What about '*r* ⊃ *p* · *q*'? Merely to tack on a further restriction—namely, (*x*) *Hx* ⊃ (*Fx* x *Gx*)—will not quite suffice to accomplish our goal here. By no means routine, the drift of the exercise at least suggests that when it comes to elementary arithmetic there may be no pressing need for numbers, and if such truths of advanced arithmetic as that 8 is even do appear to presuppose abstract entities, numbers as such are optional.

We can content ourselves with saying that for any set with 8 members there are two non-overlapping, equinumerous sets whose union is (identical with) the set. But have we not smuggled in reference to numbers by helping ourselves to this piece of jargon 'equinumerous'? Yes. Let us rather say, then, that in the case of the two sets, there is a function that correlates each member of the one set with a member of the other, again adding as provisos both that (*a*) any two members of the one set are correlated with distinct members of the other, and that (*b*) each member of the second set constitutes the value of the function for some member of the first set taken as argument.

If numbers can be dispensed with at least as much in the case of '8 is even' as in that of '5 + 7 = 12', there remains a decisive difference in our glossing of the two formulas, given that abstract entities are invoked in the one but not in the other case. Replacing numbers with any such set (and function) theoretical account is scarcely to be recommended on the ground of ontological parsimony. More to the point is the fact that, instead of taking '8 is even' to be a merely local truth (about a single abstract entity), which might well be thought to have little relevance when it comes to the physical world, our gloss on the sentence understands it rather as applying directly to any set with 8 members. The natural numbers do come into their own, however, when one undertakes to provide a semantics for the full portfolio of formulas supplied by the extended number system. According to the standard account of these matters, styled by Russell the 'logical construction' of the extra-natural numbers, one is asked to believe that on turning the pages of any treatise of physics the numeral 8 will be found therein to be systematically ambiguous. Denoting the natural number 8 on some occasions, it can be shown to denote a signed number—namely positive 8—on others, where any tendency we may have to identify the latter (positive 8) with the former (the natural number 8) is sternly rebuked. But that is only the beginning. Other occasions feature the numeral 8 as referring to the rational number 8/1, others to the real number 7.999 . . . , and still others require it to designate the corresponding complex number. Rendering '8' unambiguous in the diversified contexts in which it is used thus inevitably requires a formidable hermeneutic. How poetry revels in such ambiguity we have come richly to appreciate, though it is standardly supposed that the hard sciences, by way of sharp contrast, insist on univocity as a prime desideratum, at least in their more austere formulations. What then are we to make of this so-called rigorous approach to the extended number system?

Far from abstruse, the merits of the 'rigorous' approach positively shine forth as soon as one puzzles over so simple an equation as '$x = 5 - 8$'. That 8 cannot possibly be subtracted from 5, no mathematician of classical antiquity would hesitate to insist. Have we then in the interim discovered a proof whereby, unbeknownst to the ancients, the trick can after all be performed? That way madness lies. Wiser, the late medievals were content to denominate the negative numbers, which had only recently surfaced in some obscure, if not disreputable, fashion, *numeri ficti*, or fictitious numbers, and here again, their response was beyond reproach. It is only later, in the nineteenth century, that another tack, of much less clarity, came to be fashionable among professional mathematicians. The negative numbers are now taken to be *postulated* (magic word) in order to enable the otherwise insoluble equation '$x = 5 - 8$' to be solved. In the same vein, the rationals are postulated in order to solve '$2x = 3$', the irrationals for '$x^2 = 2$', and the imaginaries for '$x^2 = -1$'. An intellectual disaster area according to Frege, this whole approach has been memorably described by Russell as 'having all the advantages of theft over honest toil'. But even Russell respected the *motivation* underlying the postulational approach. It is at least tacitly assumed that, one way or another, one inevitably wishes to solve those insoluble equations. The wish itself being thus regarded as fully reputable, the postulationist is to be convicted merely of wishful thinking when he dispenses with the honest toil in which the standard, 'rigorous' approach exults, as it sharply distinguishes the psychological matter of motivation from the logical one of justification.

The logic of justification here is most convincingly exhibited in terms of an exercise in semantics. Take the predicate 'x is greater by 8 than y' which is satisfied by the ordered pairs $<9, 1>$, $<10, 2>$, $<11, 3>$, and so on, just as 'x is father of y' is satisfied by the pairs Peleus and Achilles, Abraham and Isaac, and so forth. As fundamental for logic as it is for grammar (and ontology), the subject–predicate relation is now found to apply not merely to one-place predicates like 'x is wise' but to n-place ($n > 1$) predicates as well, seeing that predication is just the converse of satisfaction. Just as 'wise' or 'x is wise' is predicated of Socrates, so 'father of' or 'x is father of y' can be said to be predicated of the single object that is the ordered pair $<$Abraham, Isaac$>$. Because semantics is concerned with the ontological import of various linguistic expressions, the 'semantic value' (invoking Dummett's jargon) of the proper name 'Socrates' will be Socrates, the semantic value of 'x is wise' will be (the set of) everyone who is wise, and we can even insist that the semantic value of a whole sentence must be its truth value, thereby vindicating Frege's reification of truth and falsity as objects out in the world. In much the same vein it is now argued that the semantic value of the mathematical expression 'positive 8' or 'plus 8', at any rate on those occasions when it is being used as a singular term, can only be the infinite set of ordered pairs of natural numbers that severally satisfy the predicate 'x is greater by 8 than y'. But that entails that positive 8 just is (identical with) the infinite set, while negative 8 in its turn comes to sight as the infinite set of ordered pairs, $<1, 9>$, $<2, 10>$, $<3, 11>$, and so forth, that satisfy the converse relation 'x is less by 8 than y'. For the ordered pair $<$Isaac, Abraham$>$ must not be confused with $<$Abraham, Isaac$>$, since only the former satisfies the predicate 'x is a son of y'.

How precisely does this 'logical construction' of the signed numbers out of the natural numbers and their set-theoretical spin-offs help us in subtracting 8 from 5? The question is misconceived. If the expressions '8' and '5' are taken here to denote the natural numbers 8 and 5 (and used off the cuff they can be understood in no other way), the operation is taboo quite as much for the contemporary as for the ancient mathematician. Instead, we must engage in what Quine calls semantic ascent, and ask rather what the linguistic items '8' and '5' must be taken to denote if '$x = 5 - 8$' is to be soluble. And even that is not quite right. For it is very unclear what subtracting even positive 5 from positive 8 (to choose the simplest sort of case) could possibly come to *once we direct our attention to the two infinite sets of ordered pairs of natural numbers*, one of which we are being asked to subtract from the other. Not that subtracting one set from another set need perplex us, for the intuitive sense of 'subtracting the set of Frenchmen from the set of all human beings' is perfectly clear. The trouble is that no such operation avails in the case at hand. According to the standard approach, then, it is not merely that the natural number 8 cannot be subtracted from the natural number 5; it is not even possible to subtract the signed number, positive 5, from the signed number, positive 8! The best we can hope to achieve is to 'subtract' (and here scare quotes are precisely in order) the former from the latter. Just look at what we are being asked to do. Subtraction (and here I do mean subtraction and not 'subtraction') does take place. The trouble is that the operation is performed not once but three times, and it is accordingly this threefold operation of subtraction that as a unit can qualify only as 'subtraction'. First, we pick at random some member of positive 5, say $<96, 91>$, and subtract—really subtract—91 from 96, yielding the natural number 5. Then we choose some member of positive 8, say $<847, 839>$, and subtracting the second from the first member of the ordered pair produce 8 as our result. Finally, subtraction is performed for the last time when 5 is subtracted from 8. With the natural number 3 well in hand, we proceed to 'construct' the signed number positive 3 as the set consisting of $<4, 1>$, $<5, 2>$, . . .{/}. The omnibus operation performed by us, even while involving subtraction thrice over, cannot even be said to *resemble* subtraction, for we are engaged rather in *pros hen* equivocation (recalling Aristotle) when we employ the same *word* 'subtraction' (no scare quotes here) to the domain of the signed as well as to that of the natural numbers. How one is expected to 'subtract' (scare quotes again) positive 8 from positive 5 should be evident.

If *pros hen* equivocation is one sort of rhetorical trope that comes into play, the trope of analogy is another. There are various formal features that 'subtraction' shares with subtraction, as it can be seen that while '$(x) (y) x + y = y + x$' is true in the domain of the natural numbers, '$(x) (y) x - y = y - x$' is not. Addition is thus order-indifferent, while subtraction is not. It turns out that these purely formal features, order indifference being only one such feature distinguishing addition from subtraction, carry over intact into 'addition' and 'subtraction' respectively, and it can thus be said that 'subtraction' is after all analogous to subtraction. Beyond that, the operation of 'subtraction' can even be called *subtraction* by analogy. Thanks to the interplay of these two tropes (namely, that of *pros hen* equivocation and that of analogy) which in Chapter 7 were found to fuse in the case of 'a healthy mind', the poetics of the extended number system proves to be at least as complex as the poetics of poetry itself. Ours is, however, first and foremost an ontological poetics, for our semantic ascent from things (numbers in the present case) to words (that is, numerals) has been conducted solely out of an interest in the things themselves, which are seen in the end to encompass not only the natural numbers, but infinite sets of ordered pairs of them as well.

The next step will be to 'construct' the rationals, each of which will figure also as an infinite set of ordered pairs, though not of natural, but rather of *signed* numbers. And so on with the real and complex numbers? No. The procedures whereby the extended number system is constructed lack the kind of formal unity one has a right to expect. Each of the reals emerges simply as an infinite set of rationals, in particular, the set of all the rationals less than (in the case of irrationals like $\sqrt{2}$) or equal to (in the case of rational reals) the real number in question. At the very least it is easy enough to see that each real number is uniquely determined by some such set of rationals. So the ordered pair has dropped out of the picture? No. Each complex number is found to be an ordered pair of real numbers.

Sustaining the whole system, the natural numbers themselves emerge as sets in Frege's programme, and it is here above all, in connection with his 'ontological argument' for the existence of numbers, that Frege is at once at his most ingenious and his most vulnerable. Numbers emerge as sets not by virtue of any special feature of numbers, but in connection with a novel (if disconcertingly fugitive) account of such familiar abstract entities as the shape or colour of this table, which independently take on the very unfamiliar guise of sets. Thus for Frege the shape of this table just is (identical with) the set of tables which are *similar* to it in the geometrician's sense of the word. Another, still more revealing (because unfamiliar) abstract object is found to be the direction of a line, which Frege expressly identifies with the set of lines parallel to it. Finally, by parity of reasoning, the number of F's (for any F) proves to be a set whose members are all those sets which are equinumerous with the set of F's, where 'equinumerous' is no more than a place-holder which is properly to be filled with the sort of function-theoretical account given in the second paragraph of this chapter. More perspicuously, 'the number of F's picks out a set each of whose members is a set that can be placed in one-to-one correspondence with the set of F's. Why we should believe any of these less than self-evident ontological theses regarding what shapes, directions, and numbers really are, Frege declines to say, presumably expecting us to yield to the sheer blaze of intelligibility with which we are being enlightened. Itself suggestive, the very absence of argument combined with the persistent use of mathematical concepts (similarity, parallelism, and one-to-one correspondence) invites us to look for hidden premisses to which a mathematician might be peculiarly susceptible. If the philosopher cannot easily rid himself of the conviction that the shape of a table (to press only one example) is a property not a set, he does not doubt that the mathematical counterpart of the philosopher's properties are to be found in sets. And he will readily confess that whereas the mathematician has succeeded in producing a formidable science regarding sets, the philosopher has nothing remotely comparable to show in respect to properties. That mathematics in any case supplies us with the most reliable, authoritative exercise of rationality, the philosopher is antecedently disposed to acknowledge; and it is thus to be suspected that proper shaping of these informal considerations into an argument of some power is already under way.

A further, linguistic consideration involves our projecting a tribe of people who are fortunate enough to be Fregeans by birthright. One has only to imagine an English-speaking country very much like our own, where (to shift examples) the expression 'the direction of a line' fulfils the following conditions: (*a*) it signifies by explicit fiat the set of lines parallel to it and (*b*) it plays a pragmatic role in those people's lives and science scarcely distinguishable from the one it plays in ours. That Frege's account fails to apply to *our* use of the expression, proves now to be no more than an inconvenient accident. From any suspicion that Frege's definition of 5 (as the set of all sets with 5 members) might be infected with circularity, *we* at any rate are mercifully exempt, for we are instantly alert to the fact that while the first occurrence of '5' here is substantival, the second is merely adjectival. There remains, however, the following query. On Frege's account, a distinct danger obtains that it might be the case that $4 = 5$. How can we be sure on purely a priori grounds that 4 and 5 are not both empty sets and hence identical? Well, it is precisely at this point that Frege's most dubious assumption comes into play—namely, that every concept (or predicate) has an extension (which is a set). So the guileful predicate 'x is not identical with x', by having a zero extension, assures us of an empty set; whereas, as a result, the predicate 'x is identical with an empty set' has as its extension a set with one member, and now 'x is either an empty set or a set with one member' is found to have as its extension a set with at least two members, and so on, as an infinite domain of pure sets is generated. Quite apart from any acquaintance with Russell's paradox, one need not be an outright sceptic in order to entertain serious doubts about Frege's assumption, particularly when it is advanced as a truth of straight logic that in tacit defiance of Kant's *Critique of Pure Reason* enables us by pure reason alone to execute a creation *ex nihilo* of what one can only call noumena.

15

The Myth of Closure

So central is the extended number system when it comes to the underpinnings of physics that meta-physics can never be satisfied with anything less than full clarity regarding it. Because poetics as broadly conceived has to do with the non-literal as opposed to the literal use of language, it is afforded the richest sort of opportunity to expose the rhetorical tropes in the mathematician's jargon, in the course of rendering unambiguous the plus and minus signs, as well as the numerals, which are otherwise shot through with systematic equivocation. We are left, however, with a veritable enigma, which needs to be articulated in the sharpest terms. The enigma arises in connection with the 'universally' held view that, in Frege's words, with the entry of the imaginaries into mathematics 'we reach the natural end of the domain of numbers'. Stated in realist terms, the extended number system is presumed in effect to stake out a 'natural kind' of reality. Far from 'carving reality at the joints', however, the system can be shown to feature a flagrantly gerrymandered fragment of heterogeneous reality that is hardly suited to enshrinement at the centre of a serious science like physics, not to mention a rigorous one like pure mathematics. Couched in these ultra-realist terms, the puzzle might be thought to be one that someone with more pragmatic leanings—the system works, doesn't it?—need not fret over; and in fact such a one might even look forward to exploiting it to the discomfort of the realist. Fair enough. I should be happy to have my discussion of this Rube Goldberg contraption (as the extended number system pretty much turns out to be) serve as a contribution to the quarrel between anti-realist and realist that is being waged on a broad front today. Viewing the present volume as a whole, that issue may even be felt in the end to dominate it.

The enigma arises specifically out of the interplay between formal and ontological considerations, where the one sort is associated with the so-called historical drive to closure, and the other with the so-called rigorous approach and its various batches of entities—for example, ordered pairs of natural numbers. An oft-told tale, the drive to closure is a bedtime story that even the standard approach fails to dispel, for the latter exists precisely in order to provide a sophisticated rationale for the former. Once upon a time, mathematicians were disappointed to find that they could not solve even so simple an equation as '$x + 8 = 5$' owing to that formal feature of the natural number system according to which addition is closed therein whereas subtraction is unfortunately open. How to remedy this 'defect'? Postulate the negative numbers. Even so, the equation '$2x = 3$' remains insoluble. Postulate, then, the rationals, and closure in respect to division is thereby secured. But what about '$x^2 = 2$' and '$x^2 = -1$'? Postulate the irrational and imaginary numbers, thereby achieving closure across the board. Well, not quite. Division by zero remains eternally open, but then nothing in this world can be expected to be perfect, and we must simply learn to live with a certain residual uneasiness here. If the terms 'open' and 'closed' have a technical meaning that is fairly obvious from the context, they are not without a surplus meaning of a more intuitive (as well as more dubious) variety. There is inevitably the thought that while the addition of any two natural numbers always supplies a number that lies *enclosed* within the domain, there are cases where subtracting one from another opens the domain up to a larger one that (in lazy moments one persists in supposing) encompasses the negative as well as the natural numbers.

The standard approach now urges us to distinguish between motivation and justification, where the one is supposed to be a psychological, the other a logical, matter. The motivation underlying the so-called drive to closure is conceded to be largely spurious, for no Greek mathematician ever chafed at being debarred from subtracting a larger from a smaller number; nor is it in fact true that irrationals were posited out of some hankering for a solution to '$x^2 = 2$'. In the first instance, then, the drive to closure is a historical artefact designed to explain current practice, though it proves to be an almost irresistible myth once algebra is found proceeding ahead at full speed. In retrospect, however, our task is taken to be one of supplying such sentences as (1), (2), and (3) with a semantics that will specify their truth conditions:

$$(1) \ (\exists x) \, x + 8 = 5.$$
$$(2) \ (\exists x) \, 2x = 3.$$
$$(3) \ (\exists x) \, x^2 = 2.$$

That (1) is not only false but necessarily false when (a) the numerals are taken to be proper names of natural numbers and (b) the plus sign signifies the familiar addition function featured in the arithmetic of the natural numbers, the standard approach refuses to contest. Nor does it doubt, as a linguistic point, that (*a*) and (*b*) do identify the *primary* semantic correlates (in reality) of the arithmetic expressions. Modestly enough, the rigorous approach is content to provide a secondary (and tertiary and so on) semantic gloss of (1) on which it proves to be true, and it is thus fair to say that the standard approach understands the extended number system in terms of a polymorphous semantics of systematic equivocation. In any such blaze of ambiguity, poetry might well delight; but one expects the hard sciences to be constitutionally committed to eschewing it as the merest distraction. As to why the mathematician and the physicist should be so averse to purging the arithmetic of the extended number system of all such notational equivocation (an undertaking easy enough to execute), the standard approach has nothing to say, relegating the query to the psychology of the sciences.

There are, in fact, two puzzles to be resolved. First, there is the need to explain and (probably) justify the reluctance of the hard sciences to implement the desideratum summed up in the maxim *unum nomen unum nominatum* when it comes to the extended number system. The second follows hard upon the first. On being fully clarified, the extended number system manifests itself as housing highly gerrymandered fragments of reality that fail to cohere into anything like a natural kind. No surprise, that, since the fragments were assembled in the first place on the basis of a sequence of equivocations. The surprise lies rather in the privileged role that this congeries of heterogeneous fragments enjoys in the hard sciences.

Waiving the negative (and *a fortiori* the imaginary) numbers, this second puzzle can be posed, in simplified form, regarding the Greek subsystem that in effect consists of the natural, rational, and real numbers. The Greek approach inevitably provides an instructive foil. The arithmetic of the natural numbers being seen to invite the theory of the ratios of natural numbers, one now proceeds from arithmetic to geometry when it comes specifically to the theory of rational and irrational *magnitudes*. With the rise of non-Euclidean geometries and the displacement of Euclidean geometry as an absolute thing, one has every reason to look to an arithmetic counterpart of the geometric distinction between rational and irrational magnitudes, which even in the first instance smacks of being a matter of ratios. For just as one may speak of the ratio, itself a certain relation, that obtains between 30 and 45, so, in much the same manner, there is a certain kind of 'ratio' or proportion that obtains between a line that is $\sqrt{2}$ inches long and one that is an inch long. In fact it is the independent science of proportion that the Greeks come to regard as the link between arithmetic and geometry, where the primary items quantified over in the theory are seen to be neutral as between being numbers or magnitudes. Later, in the seventeenth century, sophisticated mathematicians like John Wallis understood the new algebra expressly in terms of the Greek science of proportion; indeed, one has only to replace the last numeral, say, in the formula '30:45 :: 6:9' by the symbol x to produce an 'equation' whose solubility *we* can assert in a formula, (4) below, which positively exhibits how Frege's logic supervenes upon algebra, which in turn supervenes on Greek proportion theory.

$$(4) \quad (\exists x) \ 30{:}45 :: 6{:}x.$$

No such clarity attaches to the extended number system, however, whether taken straight, with its equivocations, or as rendered unambiguous along the lines of the rigorous approach.

That each rational number or ratio of natural numbers (they come to the same thing) answers to an infinite set of ordered pairs of natural numbers seems obvious enough. Again, it is obvious that each real number in its turn is uniquely associated with an infinite set of rational numbers, and in fact one has every right to insist that $\sqrt{2}$ being 1.4142 . . . just is identical with $1 + 4/10 + 1/100 + 4/1,000 + \ldots$. Why the standard approach is debarred from construing a real number as an infinite *sum* of rationals needs to be clearly understood. Any such (irrational) sum in the literal sense of the word only makes sense when geometry, broadly taken to apply to the continuous magnitudes of time as well as space, comes into play. Notice in particular that $\sqrt{2}$ as $1 + 4/10 + 1/100 + \ldots$ presupposes a unit of measurement that is infinitely divisible; hence the need for continuous magnitude. But the standard approach is purely arithmetic in the Greek sense of 'arithmetic', which precisely contrasts it with geometry by way of the distinction between the discrete and the continuous. Although Aristotle in the *Categories* is prepared to take the category of quantity as a genus that divides into the two species of the discrete and the continuous, elsewhere he recognizes that the division is largely factitious in so far as it purports to yield natural kinds that are properly co-ordinate, conflating indeed the purely arithmetic 'How many?' with the geometric 'How much?', as if there were some general item that the word 'quantity' univocally designates that is to be specifically addressed in terms of the one query or the other.

One has now only to imagine a disembodied spirit confined to quantifying over an infinite domain of discrete items—for example, jokes. If in some cases a joke may be divisible naturally enough into two or three or even four 'equal' parts, the notion of equality here is slippery at best, and infinite divisibility is not to be countenanced in the general case. The unit as such is thus taken to be indivisible in arithmetic, as in set theory, and though each rational number does find application in our infinite domain of jokes (for example, 17/19ths of these 38 jokes), infinite sums of rationals, particularly when they constitute irrationals, fail to be so much as intelligible. Content then to 'identify' each real number with an associated set of rationals, the standard approach elects in particular the whole solid block of rationals less than the real in question. The geometric counterpart to this move is especially illuminating. Suppose that the only points on the line antecedently recognized by us are the rational ones. Can we prove the existence of irrationals? I mean apart from drawing on specifically geometric resources like the Pythagorean theorem. Well, consider all the rational points to the left of $\sqrt{2}$. Put quite like that, we do seem to be begging the question. Following Dedekind, we envisage all the rationals whose squares are less than 2, contrasting that set of points with the set of rationals whose squares are greater than 2, against the background of the famous proof that there is no rational $\sqrt{2}$. That there is at least, and indeed at most, one point separating the two sets, namely $\sqrt{2}$, might well be termed the Dedekindean intuition understood as being irreducibly geometric in character.

Notice that even if one chooses to resist the intuition, perhaps merely by suspending judgement as to the existence of the putative point, the line segment constituted by the first set of points must be conceded to be $\sqrt{2}$ units long. Thus, even in the absence of irrational points, irrational magnitudes can be proved to exist! It is imperative that this truth be stressed, for there is a kind of creeping anti-realism in the philosophy of science that, even while acknowledging the rational points on a line, supposes that irrationals are a mere convenience postulated in order to round out the system. I regret to say that even Quine can be found to write that 'no measurement could be too accurate to be accommodated by a rational number but we admit the extras [i.e. irrationals] to simplify our computations and generalizations'.[1]

Abstracting from its geometrical applications, the (disambiguated) extended number system emerges like a gerrymandered map that represents Alaska, Wisconsin, and Mexico in the greatest detail but absolutely nothing else. One such country consists of the natural numbers. Another (sticking to the Greek subsystem) is the rational realm featuring ordered pairs of natural numbers, which might lead one to expect ordered triples, quadruples, and, in general, all the finite, if not the infinite, sequences of such. But no. It is the ordered pair alone that is being arbitrarily singled out. Finally, there is the realm of *certain* infinite sets of (infinite sets of) those ordered pairs, the solid blocks of rationals. Why we should have any special interest in these as opposed to the scattered sets, can be explained only by

[1] L. E. Hahn and P. A. Schilpp, eds. *The Philosophy of W. V. Quine* (LaSalle: Open Court, 1986), p. 400.

way of recourse to either geometry or the myth of closure. Cut off
from the first as a principled point of self-denial, one might be
forgiven for retreating to the second in hugger-mugger fashion;
for, while the standard approach undertakes to 'rationalize' the
extended number system, it cannot possibly dispense with the
myth so long as the system remains firmly in place, providing
the underlying framework of the hard sciences. If it should now
be suggested that our map of mathematical reality can be properly
filled out by recognizing the regions that emerge on the strength
of the negative and imaginary numbers, I can only reply: look
and see. I submit that, even on being so eked out, the map will be
quite as ontologically gerrymandered as before. Thus, at the last
stage, ordered pairs (of reals) but not ordered triples or
quadruples are once more invidiously chosen to ground the new
domain. And though infinite sets of (ordered pairs of) complex
numbers are an inevitable by-product of the system, they fail to be
correspondingly honoured as 'numbers'—itself a systematically
ambiguous word—thanks to being supernumerary when it comes
to achieving the spurious goal of closure.

In the absence of the myth of closure, the extended number
system simply disintegrates into disparate fragments of reality,
held together in the first place only by a cluster of equivocations.
The fragments being real enough, the standard approach succeeds on its own terms in altogether eschewing the postulation of
fictitious entities, and its pretensions in that regard remain
unimpugned by any of my remarks. Hence the illusion of much
more clarity than in fact obtains, when, in the end, one continues
to rely implicitly on the myth of closure, if only as a mnemonic
device for conjuring up whatever sort of 'number'—natural,
signed, rational, real, or complex—the context at hand, practical
or theoretical, may require. Why anything so factitious as this
congeries of fragments should (deserve to) remain in place by way
of constituting the underlying framework of the hard sciences
emerges in these pages as an enigma that I have been at great
pains to articulate. Put simply in terms of sentences, and
abstracting from all merely historical, considerations, why are
such sentences as '$(\exists x)\ x + 8 = 5$' and '$(\exists x)\ x^2 = -1$', not to
mention '$(\exists x)\ 2x = 3$' and '$(\exists x)\ x^2 = 2$', *all* of which come out as

false when glossed in terms of their primary semantics, assigned a secondary semantics in the hard sciences that renders them true? Why the systematic ambiguity, no appeal to the myth of closure being allowed?

One can, of course, through orienting oneself entirely by the complex numbers, insist that all four sentences are unambiguously true. But notice the consequence. The Greek mathematician says that the sentence '$(\exists x)\, x + 8 = 5$' is false, and it is not to be doubted that, given the meaning he assigns to ' $+$ ', '8', and '5', he is right. So in the hard sciences at any rate, are *we* committed to using those expressions across the board with different meanings? An implausible suggestion, whether intended in a *de facto* or a *de jure* mode. When we agree with the Greek mathematician that the sentence '$(\exists x)\, x + 5 = 8$' *is* unambiguously true, we cannot be expected to confer on either the plus sign or the numerals a novel meaning of our own. We cannot but want to say what he says and in the very way he says it. Invested with an elastic, polymorphous semantics, our extended number system is rather to be viewed as a kind of algebraic accordion. If the natural numbers remain to the end not merely non-expendable but absolutely privileged, the real numbers I take to be incontestably second in importance, for it is they that specifically address the continuous magnitudes of space, time, and motion *qua* continuous. Understood in terms of infinite sums of rationals, which (as we have seen) cannot be accommodated by the standard approach, these magnitudes are inevitably featured in meta-physics.

Poetics being taken to provide us with a hermeneutic designed to gloss sentences in terms of the distinction between literal and non-literal, it is scarcely surprising that the poetics of the extended number system should disclose it to be constituted in no merely accidental fashion by a myth, seeing that myth, metaphor, and poetry are presumably closely akin to one another. Demythologizing the hard sciences, which can scarcely refrain from conjuring with the myth, proves thus to be one of the tasks of meta-physics. My success in that regard has, however, been very limited, for the myth of closure continues to pose for us an enigma that I have failed to resolve.

16

Ordered Pairs

In our relentless drive toward total clarity, we should be inevitably, if perhaps venially, delinquent if we were simply to take as unproblematic the role of ordered pairs in the logical construction of the extended number system. And even apart from that role, there are at least three considerations that encourage us to address ordered pairs as such. Ordered pairs and, more generally, *sequences* (taken to encompass ordered triples, quadruples, and so on) have been seen to figure in the logic, semantics, and ontology of predication, as when we say that 'x is the father of y' is predicated of $<$Abraham, Isaac$>$. Predication itself being arguably the deepest theme of metaphysics, Frege has been found to understand it in terms of objects (as subjects) and functions (as predicates). It may thus be a source of puzzlement that I have hitherto refrained from expediting the discussion by adopting the widespread view that a function is simply an infinite set of ordered pairs. The set-theoretical counterpart of the successor function $f(x) = x + 1$ being the set consisting of $<1, 2>$, $<2, 3>$, $<3, 4>$, and so forth, sets are readily available to go proxy for functions if, like most philosophers, one feels more at ease with the one than with the other. Finally, with specific reference to the ontology of events as they emerged in Chapter 6 in connection with the logic of adverbs, Jaegwon Kim has proposed that each event is to be identified with an ordered triple. Thus the sinking of the *Titanic* consists of (1) a certain substance, namely the *Titanic*, (2) a certain property, namely that of sinking, and (3) the precise date on which the *Titanic* sank. I mention Kim's 'logical construction' of events out of substances, properties, and times merely as an example of the role of sequences in contemporary ontology.

That functions are just infinite sets of ordered pairs is so much of a commonplace today that Frege's protest is likely to go unheeded. One is guilty of the most profound category mistake (and here Frege is as Aristotelian as Ryle) if one confuses a set, which is inevitably an object, with a function, which in its incompleteness answers to the gappiness of a predicate, as in 'x is wise'. An Aristotelic as well as a Platonist (and it is precisely this double role that peculiarly equips Frege to launch the renewal of classical metaphysics in our time), Frege does not hesitate to convict Plato himself of just that category mistake, as he is led up the garden path from (1) to (2) to (3) and so on.

(1) Socrates is wise.
(2) Socrates has (the property of) wisdom.
(3) Socrates and wisdom satisfy the 'x has y' relation—call it R_1.
(4) R_1, Socrates, and wisdom satisfy the R_2 relation—namely, 'x is satisfied by y and z'.

Arguing in effect that the semantic content (= ontological import) of (1) is explicitly specified by (2), Plato is open to the charge that by parity of reasoning the semantic content of (2), and *a fortiori* of (1) as well, is explicitly specified by (3), which in *its* turn . . . Accordingly, Frege insists, the content of none of these predicates—for example, 'x has wisdom'—can be taken to be supplied by any object whatsoever. Music to the ears of the nominalist, the argument is by no means intended by Frege to show that (1) commits us to only one entity, Socrates. A second, extra-mental, Platonic item is indicated by the predicate 'x is wise'; only it is not an object, but a function. Although I have myself proposed that the logical form of (1) can be exhibited as 'Something, namely Socrates, is something, namely wise', it is not quite the case that two things or two somethings are involved, but rather that two senses of the word 'something' are being put in play. A familiar piece of philosophical jargon, the locution 'predicating something of something' can now come to look very dubious. For the nominalist has traditionally agreed with the Platonist that (1) involves a certain object's being predicated of Socrates. They differ only as to what that object is, the one insisting that it is no more than the mere word 'wise', the other that it can be no less than wisdom itself. The piece of jargon presumably answers to what in the vernacular is expressed by 'saying something is something', but this latter, by featuring a second-order as well as a first-order use of 'something', relieves us from the necessity of supposing that any object whatever is being 'predicated' of Socrates. To the vernacular idiom in its turn I am quite prepared to believe with Frege that the mathematician's jargon regarding functions answers still more deeply, though for us non-mathematicians there is the lurking suspicion that undertaking to explain predication in terms of functions could only be a case of *obscurum per obscurius*. The specifically idiomatic feature of the mathematician's jargon is betrayed by the fact that though 12 may be said to be a function of 6 (alluding to the doubling function, say) '12' cannot be detached by way of some putative rule of simplification from its immediate context and thereby taken to signify a function all on its own. Non-detachability, as a criterion of the idiomatic, has been illustrated by one waggish philosopher, who remarks that if it is raining cats and dogs, one is not thereby licensed to infer that there are poodles in the street. Arguably a talisman reserved to initiates of the mathematical coterie, functions cannot simply be taken to answer *directly* to anything in reality, though (again) this ruling is easy enough for a mere philosopher to propose when conversing with *his* coterie. Under the banner of Quine's maxim 'Explication is elimination', the philosopher may now even choose to view himself as eliminating functions across the board, in favour of infinite sets of ordered pairs, which are thus pressed into service to fill the vacuum.

Strikingly, Quine's maxim surfaces in the course of the section of *Word and Object* entitled 'The ordered pair as philosophical paradigm', where it turns out that ordered pairs, being themselves only mythical entities, require other entities to go proxy for them! The consequences are not negligible. For if functions are replaced by ordered pairs, ordered pairs prove also to be junked in their turn. Why ordered pairs are now thought to be themselves only mythical entities, can be brought out as follows. Although a set-like item, the ordered pair < Paris, London > cannot be identified with the ordered pair < London, Paris >, by contrast with the set {Paris, London}, which is identical with the set {London, Paris}. The difference within the two ordered pairs has to do with which city comes first. For someone travelling across Europe from south to north, Paris comes first. But if that expresses too literal-minded an approach, London may rank before Paris in population, while Paris doubtless ranks before it in the quality of its restaurants. Maybe, then, the ordered pair < Paris, London > is none other than the set consisting of (a) Paris, (b) London, and (c) (the set of) all the respects in which Paris ranks ahead of London. But then that ordered pair will consist of at least three and perhaps even infinitely many members. After all, if the average man need not be a man, why assume that a so-called ordered pair has only two members? Dialectical considerations of that sort have persuaded philosophers like myself that even God could not tell us what ordered pairs really are. What to do then? Cynically opportunistic as it may well appear, the standard approach today is conservative enough to mimic ordered pairs by doubleton sets. Thus Norbert Wiener construes the ordered pair < Paris, London > as the set consisting of (*a*) the unit set whose only member is Paris and (*b*) the doubleton set whose members are London and the empty set. The trick here is to regard the unordered set as having 'inscribed' within it a 'code' that enables us to recognize which of the two cities comes first and which second in the make-believe ordered pair that the unordered set is simulating. Alternatively, one may with Kuratowski choose to construe the ordered pair < Paris, London > as the set consisting of (*a*) the unit set whose only member is Paris and (*b*) the doubleton set consisting of Paris and London. Again, given the members of the set in any order, one has a code at one's disposal that selects Paris as 'preceding' London, though precedence here is the merest fiction. So absurdly artificial is the whole procedure that one may feel that reality must of necessity get lost in the shuffle; for we are even to be seen tossing a coin to determine which of the two, Wiener or Kuratowski sets, will henceforth qualify as ordered pairs—that is, henceforth qualify as referents for the expression 'ordered pair'—in the new idiolect that we shall be adopting when we discuss reality pure and simple.

In the first instance, we may tentatively suppose that such discussions will consist principally of straight physics, augmented, however, by our rational reconstruction of the extended number system where (let us say) the real numbers are regarded as infinite sets of infinite sets of ordered pairs, construed as Kuratowski sets, of natural numbers. Not that anyone could seriously be supposed to *think* the real numbers expressly in those Byzantine terms. Our actual thinking will continue to be conducted in terms of the unreconstructed ordered pair, as when we say that '*x* is the father of *y*' is satisfied by that single object which is the ordered pair < Abraham, Isaac >, whose proxy in our austere ontology figures as {{Abraham}, {Abraham, Isaac}} where it is to be noticed that angle brackets are used for ordered pairs, and curly brackets are used for sets. For it is only the latter object that really *satisfies* the dyadic predicate in our idiolect, satisfaction being defined strictly (in semantics) as a very non-intuitive relation that a peculiar sort of set bears to a predicate. By translating the sentences in the Book of Science into our new idiolect, realists are entitled now to insist that the sentences are true after all, though if they are asked to explain precisely what 'a force of $\sqrt{2}$ ft. lbs.' means in our idiolect, they can only lead the questioner along step by step as he is brought to rehearse our recent discussions. That same expression proves to be woefully underdetermined as to both sense and reference when it is mouthed by the working physicist who has not had the benefit of our Quinean reconstruction of physical discourse. Although his *use* of the expression will not differ from our own along any pragmatic dimension (here understood to extend all the way to the highest reaches of theoretical physics), the expression as he understands it can only be scorned by us as radically defective on the ontological front. In effect, then, we Quineans are conceding to the anti-realist that mathematical and physical discourse taken raw is to be understood in terms of its pragmatic, rather than its ontological, import. Again, when the working mathematician proves (as one says) that $\sqrt{3}$ is greater than $\sqrt{2}$, we can only protest that these expressions '$\sqrt{3}$' and '$\sqrt{2}$' fail to achieve any determinate reference in his use of them. Appearances to the contrary, then, he has proved nothing. Implausible? Of course. The merest 'shadow' or 'image' of a proof is all that results from his efforts, as Plato would say.

It is not only pure mathematics that admits of logical construction: witness Kim's construction of events, though Whitehead is the classic case. Having in effect explicated each point in space or space-time by noticing that it is uniquely determined by the set of all the (inevitably overlapping) regions, both large and small, that contain it, A. N. Whitehead memorably proposed the 'elimination' of all such points from physics in favour of their associated sets of regions. Thus 'the center of gravity of the Earth' will cease to denote a point as such, but will designate instead the set of regions that contain it, in the fashion of Chinese boxes. Distinguishing one such set from another 'neighbouring' set inevitably involves peering down into the small end of the 'funnel'. This 'elimination' of points is no less suitably described as their 'logical construction' out of (sets of) regions, and this very ambiguity—is it explication or elimination?—invites us to consider two theories of the world, T_1 and T_2, following a recent seminar at Harvard conducted jointly by Hilary Putnam, Goodman, and Quine. T_1 and T_2 differ in only one respect. Where T_1 quantifies over points as well as their corresponding sets of regions, T_2 quantifies only over the regions and their sets, going so far as to even expressly endorse the formula '$\sim (\exists x)$ x is a point'. Could God tell us which of these two logically incompatible theories is the true one? Although the logical realist (as we may style him) will not hesitate to answer in the affirmative, most realists to whom I have posed the query are found to be shaken by it. In the same vein, consider now T_3, which quantifies only over points and sets of points, endorsing the sentence '$\sim (\exists x)$ x is a region of space'. If T_2 trades on the fact that each point is determined in bull's-eye fashion by a set of regions, T_3 appeals still more directly to the fact that a set of points can correspond so closely to a region that some of the less astute among us will be found to ask in all candour. 'But isn't a region just the set of points within it?' Contrasting T_3 with T_2—that is to say, an ontology of points with one of regions, where rationalists have been happier with the former and empiricists with the latter—is there a 'fact of the matter' as to which of these pragmatically equivalent theories truly describes the world? Here, then, is the entering wedge of the new idealism, which is more trendily referred to as anti-realism. Not only points and regions, but everything else as well is held to be a 'construction' of the mind, and to ask now whether anything in reality corresponds to these constructions is deemed to be otiose.

Part IV

17

ZF Intuition

Discussing the deepest kind of philosophic insight into his transcendent Forms, Plato writes in his Seventh Letter that 'it does not at all admit of verbal expression like other studies but as a result of continued application to the subject itself and communion therewith, it is brought to birth in the soul on a sudden, as light that is kindled by a leaping spark, and therafter it nourishes itself' (341c–d). A *locus classicus* regarding rational intuition, the text makes clear precisely how Plato's variety differs from the more familiar sort associated with Descartes and Kant that pertains to obvious truths like '2 + 2 = 4' immediately evident to us all. Rational intuition of the Platonic kind is activated only against a background of continued application to such highly dialectical studies as these chapters have undertaken, and though it is widely believed that what Plato is gesturing towards must be very mysterious, a relatively accessible instance of it appears to be available today in the form of so-called ZF intuition, with which the more visionary devotees of Zermelo–Fraenkel set theory credit themselves.

Content in these pages to explain the ZF *conception* of sets, I can only trust that the intuition will vouchsafe itself as a bonus, though it must be stressed that as in the case of Plato's Forms, so here in that of the mathematician's sets—the kinship between the two has not gone unremarked—'continued application to the subject itself', even to the point of total immersion in the vicissitudes of set theory, Russell's paradox above all, is almost penitentially demanded by our ZF devotees. Having been engaged in recent chapters in an ambitious project that realist and idealist alike might almost be tempted to characterize, in their different ways, as the logical construction of the world itself, we can hardly dispense with the obligation to defend the sponsoring notion, that of set, against the challenge posed by Russell. Specifically, what we want to know is precisely what it is about sets as such, sets *qua* sets, that precludes there being a set of all sets that are not members of themselves. Insight being above all what we seek, Zermelo would seem to be the least promising source to consult; for he was positively ostentatious in insisting that his was no more than a home remedy, suited to the needs of the working mathematician on the most pedestrian level. After conceding at the outset of his paper of 1908 that up to then no fully satisfactory solution to Russell's paradox had been found, Zermelo observes that 'it does not today seem permissible any more to assign to any arbitrary logically definable concept' (notably that expressed by the predicate 'x is not a member of x') 'a "set" or "class" as its extension'. What to do? Although 'Cantor's original definition of a "set" as a "comprehension of definite distinct objects of our intuition or our thought into a whole" . . . certainly requires some limitation . . . no one has yet succeeded in replacing it by another definition, equally simple, that is not exposed to any such doubt.' Notice that what is 'required' here Zermelo reports as being unavailable, at any rate as of 'now'; it is thus very much in a spirit of second best, if not as a provisional stopgap, that he undertakes in piecemeal fashion to collect seven reliable axioms none of which would strike the advanced mathematicians of his day as particularly novel.[1] Typical is the power set axiom, which for any set K guarantees the existence of another set, K_1, whose members are all the subsets of K. Just about the only axiom worth lingering over is the separation axiom, if only because it exploits the notion of a property, which one supposes to be precisely what sets are designed to replace. This axiom states that for any set K and any property F, there is a set K_1 whose members are all the members of K that are F, the point being of course—though this is tacit—that properties are never allowed to determine sets on their own, but only when they serve to separate the members of a given set into a new one. Strikingly—though this has gone largely unnoticed—there is no axiom of ZF that allows us to insist that there is a set of all men, especially if we allow that there may be

---

[1] An especially useful discussion of these axioms, taken one by one, I found in G. T. Kneebone, *Mathematical Logic and Foundations of Mathematics* (D. van Nostrand Company, London: 1963), pp. 287–92.

infinitely many scattered throughout the universe! So much is ZF designed for the professional mathematician engaged exclusively in pure mathematics that any such extramural considerations are felt to be *hors de combat*.

Although a certain fastidiousness is operative in the separation axiom, one looks in vain—I mean apart from the advantages conferred on us by hindsight—for any omnibus principle, let alone intuition, presiding over Zermelo's seven axioms, each of which appears to have been judiciously selected on its own individual merits. In retrospect, however, one is struck by the fact that the power set and separation axioms (looking no further) share the important characteristic of allowing a new set to emerge as a spin-off from an old one. One also notices that caution is by no means the overriding consideration one had been led to expect. Witness the highly controversial axiom of choice that Zermelo guilefully slips into his workaday system. Only a few years before, French mathematicians, in their famous '*cinq lettres*', refused to accept Zermelo's 'proof'—based on the axiom of choice which he conjured up for the nonce (no one had ever heard of it)—that there exists a well-ordering of the real numbers. One axiom in ZF especially, supplied by Abraham Fraenkel, has been seen by Charles Parsons to encapsulate the ZF conception of a set. This is the foundation axiom, which rules out 'ungrounded' sets with the following open-ended character . . . $K_3 \in K_2 \in K_1 \in K$. In particular, there can be no set of everything that is not a man. For with regard to such a set, call it 'K', the following would obtain: . . . $K \in K \in K$. In Platonic terms, although there is a form, or *eidos*, 'man', thanks to which all men are men by virtue of participating in it, there is presumably no form 'not man' or 'other than man', which is not to deny that Plato is keenly sensitive to the role of the indeterminate *heteron*, or other, in our thinking. The many things, then, that satisfy the predicate '*x* is not a man' fail to constitute a set according to ZF. More directly relevant to Frege's programme can be seen to be the truth of the following:

(1) $\sim (\exists x)\ (y)\ y$ is a set with exactly 2 members $\supset y \in x$.

Assume that in defiance of (1) there is a set, Q, of all doubbleton sets. Thanks to the pairing axiom there is then another set, Q_1, consisting of Q and Paris, and the foundation axiom is violated thus: . . . $Q_1 \epsilon Q \epsilon Q_1 \epsilon Q$. Notice that Q is precisely the set with which Frege identifies the number 2, and in the absence of Q there is surely no other set that could be suggested as a plausible substitute. So for a Quine, there simply are no numbers. Quantifying over sets as the only abstract entities in his austere ontology, Quine can continue to conjure with the natural numbers, but only as convenient fictions. What then becomes of our logical construction of the extended number system *out of* the natural numbers? Well, the standard approach here is to indulge anew in the harmless fakery with which we are familiar through dealing with ordered pairs. Zermelo's suggestion is as good as any, though we shall give it a linguistic twist. Let the inscriptions '0', '1', '2', and so on henceforth designate in our idiolect the following items respectively: the empty set, the unit set of the empty set, the unit set of that, and so forth. Despite being the proper names of certain pure sets, the number-words will continue to be used by us, on the pragmatic front, as before, for counting and the rest. It must be confessed, however, that this blatantly factitious exercise is only taking us away from our goal—namely, insight, let alone intuition—since merely drawing out the logical consequences of the foundation axiom is only marginally better when what we want is some deep rationale for accepting it.

Widely regarded today as the iterative (or cumulative) conception of a set,[2] the ZF approach is still more illuminatingly characterized as an ordinal conception, drawing on the distinction between ordinal and cardinal numbers. There are sets on the first level (for example, the set of men), sets on the second level, the third level, and so on, each set being understood to emerge at a particular level that may be assigned an ordinal number as its index. Decisive here is the insistence that the members of any set must all be found at some lower level. The trouble indeed with Q is that one of its members—namely, Q_1—emerges at a level higher than Q, in fact, the very next level. Sets are thus seen to *supervene* on their members, as they are not merely constituted by but

---

[2] See in particular George Boolos, 'The Iterative Conception of Set', *Journal of Philosophy*, 68 (1971): 215–32.

supervenient on them as well. The distinction is of some use here. Posit a set of all sets. Constituted by its members, it will fail, however, to supervene on each and every one of them, if only because it could hardly be supposed to supervene on itself. Pursuing this thought, it must be added that if the '$x \in y$' relation is taken to be a special (albeit converse) case of the more general 'y supervenes on x' relation to which we are looking for light, our understanding of what a set is supposed to be ceases to be a local affair, and it is thus not the set *qua* set but rather the set *qua* supervenient entity that succeeds in conjuring away Russell's paradox.

I am assuming here that we have some independent grasp of the supervenience relation, quite apart from set theory, for it is only on that basis that we can draw on the following analogy. As a nation is constituted by and supervenient on its citizens, as a man is constituted by and supervenient on the molecules that compose him, as a molecule . . ., as an atom . . ., so is a set constituted by and supervenient on its members. That the constitution and supervenience relations are scarcely distinguishable is suggested by the following consideration. How something—for example, the set of all sets—could be constituted by various entities one of which is itself, appears to be just as impossible—in fact, it seems to be the very same phenomenon—as that it should supervene upon them.

But for one difficulty I would be tempted to conclude that what the ZF conception of a set finally comes to ontologically is just this notion of supervenience or constitution. The difficulty is this. According to the supervenience theory, it is senseless to suppose that there could be an empty set. There is simply nothing for an empty set to be constituted by, just as there is nothing for it to supervene upon; and yet if one takes the iterative or even the ordinal conception of a set in the standard way (not to mention the historical fact that the empty set has never been supposed to be, like the axiom of choice, an optional feature of ZF that one was free to discard), the empty set is securely lodged on level 1. It is also worth mentioning that Zermelo's miscellaneous axiom of elementary sets provides for the empty set, along with unit sets and the pairing axiom. Nor is the empty set without important work to do when it comes to the natural numbers and, more generally, the extended number system, as we have just noticed. Speaking openly as a metaphysician, I am prepared to assert that our ZF enthusiasts, who have never hesitated to endorse the empty set, are not to be believed when they plume themselves on having a deep, coherent intuition into what sets are all about. These are fighting words. Ever since the now almost legendary Kurt Gödel wrote that Russell's paradox was 'a very serious problem, not for mathematics, however, but rather for logic and epistemology', the ZF conception has been cherished above all as the mathematician's response to a philosopher's quandary. Tension between mathematician and philosopher having already surfaced earlier in these pages, notably at the end of Chapter 9, the present discussion is expressly intended as one further bout in a continuing argument between philosopher and mathematician. A mere word may be said to divide us. Although one says casually enough that ZF requires every set to be grounded, there is a strong, as well as a weak, use of the word that needs to be relished. The empty set is grounded only in a weak, formal, even negative use of the word: there is nothing antecedent to it upon which it supervenes. It remains for *us* ungrounded, in that it is seen to consist of nothing and to float free without a proper foundation. No wonder that the mathematician should wish to view his enterprise as being truly ungrounded, as resting on nothing outside itself, or that the philosopher should insist on an extra-mathematical grounding of it. If the metaphysical conception of sets as supervenient entities welcomes the ZF approach as a first approximation to the truth, it is even prepared to give full marks to a mathematician for anticipating it. Dedekind, then, was exactly right when he rejected the empty set on the ground that sets are constituted by their antecedent members; and in an eirenic spirit let me then denominate my own as the Dedekindean approach.

In the precise sense of the term, sets are to be recognized as emergent entities. How life and, above all, mind are to be understood as emerging out of a purely physical universe has long been acknowledged as one of the central issues of philosophy, but the issue has not been grasped in its full generality as applying to sets.

One has been tempted to urge that in sharp contrast with life and mind, sets can be positively seen to be logically and hence trivially emergent items whose existence is entailed by their members. As a point of strict logic, then, is the following a formally valid argument? '$(\exists x)(\exists y)$ x is a rock $\cdot$ y is a rock $\cdot$ $\sim(x = y)$. Therefore, $(\exists x)(\exists y)(\exists z) \sim(x = y) \cdot x \in z \cdot y \in z$.' Well yes, if set theory is to count as logic, but Quine has already convinced us of the contrary, on the ground that two things can never entail three things. Even mountains are to be viewed as emergent entities, though here again it is widely, if tacitly, assumed that from a description of the world in terms of such relatively low-level items as rocks, trees, and soil, one can in effect deduce the higher-level existence of mountains. I do not believe it. The thought here is that the word 'mountain' acquires a non-zero extension simply on the strength of rocks, trees, and so on being suitably related to one another, as if any such verbal sleight of hand could logically suffice to add a single object to one's ontology. One appeals to the meaning of the word 'mountain' as one's rule of inference, even though no such rule is recognized by professional logicians. Call this, indeed, 'the linguistic fallacy'; it will be found to be endemic to much contemporary philosophy. One can only be grateful to Peter van Inwagen for challenging it. It is not merely life and mind that come to sight logically as meta-physical, but sets and mountains as well, particularly after one has digested Democritus's profound, though virtually unknown, dictum (reported by Aristotle in *Metaphysics*, 7. 13. 1039a10) to the effect that 'one thing cannot be made out of two nor two out of one', in which he is presumably denying that his ultimate atoms can ever conspire together to constitute some new thing, be it a mountain or anything else.

If, thanks to their utter purity, sets can be seen to be exemplary when it comes to the whole issue of emergent objects, our own intuition into the ontology of sets has been derived largely from a more general sort of inquiry into supervenience as such. Wresting sets away from the parochial attention of the mathematician and back to the synoptic vision of the philosopher, I remain grateful to ZF for its insistence on the specific feature of ordinality, which needs, however, to be richly savoured for its strangeness, given that set theory is virtually to be identified with the theory of cardinality, as opposed to ordinality. Does the ZF intuition into cardinality presuppose, then, an antecedent and unthematic access to ordinality? If the cardinal numbers 1, 2, 3, and so on supply the answer to the question 'How many?', the ordinals are indicated whenever we speak of what comes first, second, third, and so forth in some ordering. One approaches the natural numbers in terms of either ordinality (Peano) or cardinality (set theory). Set theory despises ordinality, hence the elimination of the ordered pair as such and its replacement by the grotesque substitutes proposed by Wiener and Kuratowski. Another sign of that contempt is evidenced by our statement that the so-called natural order of the natural numbers has no privileged status. Instead of treating them as the ω sequence 1, 2, 3, 4, . . ., why not assign them an $\omega + 5$ ordinality—for example, 6, 7, 8, 9, 10, 11, . . ., 1, 2, 3, 4, 5? Or even a 2ω ordinality—for example, 1, 3, 5, 7, . . ., 2, 4, 6, . . . That, at any rate, is characteristic of set theory when taken up front. Peano, by contrast, is so impressed by the natural numbers as being definitive of a progression—namely, ω ordinality—that for him any progression can go proxy for the natural numbers, even 2, 4, 6, 8, . . . or Zermelo's sequence of pure sets. Conversely, Zermelo—and it is his replacement of the natural numbers by a progression that provides the clue—may be suspected of importing into the secret foundations of set theory Peano's fix on ordinality.

Supervenience and ordinality each being seen to strike a deep vein when taken by itself, it is the fusion of the two that invests ZF intuition with its noetic allure. With regard to both components of the intuition, we found that we had to go outside set theory in order to secure an independent grip on them. But that is precisely what one expects from a mode of inquiry that can be seen to be very much on the way to first principles.

18

The Synthetic A Priori

On being challenged by a journalist in 1931 to condense into a single sentence the controversial doctrines of the logical positivists, one of their spokesmen, Moritz Schlick, responded, 'There is no synthetic a priori'. Against Kant's insistence that metaphysical propositions must be both synthetic (a logical point) and a priori (an epistemological point), Schlick's reply was designed to sum up the grounds of the positivists for rejecting metaphysics. Basically, the grounds were Kant's, but with this difference. Kant took Euclidean geometry to be an obvious source of synthetic a priori truths, and he was content merely to insist that while a ready explanation of that fact can be found in our spatial intuition—one can just (so to speak) *see* that through a point outside a straight line one and only one parallel to it can be drawn—no such faculty is available to the philosopher. Accordingly, the philosopher needs a special justification, which Kant in fact professes to supply; only it turns out that the synthetic a priori truths peculiar to philosophy fail to apply to things in themselves, thereby being of no use to the metaphysician, who is left bankrupt.

Too complicated to command anyone's ready assent, Kant's case against metaphysics subsequently came to be beautifully simplified with the discrediting of the putative intuitions on which Euclidean geometry relies, as non-Euclidean geometries came to be regarded as fully acceptable. Intuition came to acquire a bad name across the board, not least in ethics, and the synthetic a priori—a contentious notion at best from the moment Kant introduced it—ceased to be reputable. So much for ancient history. A new era arises; oblivion sets in; and lo! intuition is reaffirmed, again in connection with mathematics, not indeed geometry, but now ZF set theory. Moreover, if Euclidean geometry in the past often served the metaphysician as a model for his own enterprise, notably in the case of Spinoza, whose system is expressly cast *more geometrico*, set theory, by contrast, can be seen to be metaphysics itself. The opportunity to reopen this whole issue of the synthetic a priori, which has scarcely been mentioned since the forties, I could hardly be expected to ignore. Why Kant insisted on the synthetic a priori as absolutely critical for the future prospects of metaphysics can be readily deduced from two premises. One has already been discussed in Chapter 5, where Kant was seen to denigrate analytic propositions as suited to play only a secondary role of clarification in any substantive inquiry. The other premiss consists in the reflection that a posteriori truths are properly to be verified by the empirical scientist, not the armchair philosopher. If the first premiss requires of a properly metaphysical proposition that it be synthetic, the second proceeds to invest it with an a priori status, though the combination of the two conditions can readily appear to involve (as Kant was eager to emphasize) a shot-gun marriage between incompatibles. How Quine deftly met Kant's challenge will be recalled from Chapter 6, where the metaphysical proposition 'There are abstract entities' was vindicated on an a posteriori basis. More perspicuous in that line is the Kim–Davidson argument, which can be reconstructed as follows. Granted that the nominalist is right when he insists that the truth of 'Tom is walking' commits us only to the existence of Tom, he turns out to be mistaken when it comes to the only slightly more complicated statement 'Tom is walking slowly'. The a posteriori truth of 'Tom is walking slowly' is found—by a tricky consideration of logic itself—to entail a second entity—namely, a certain event—and since each event is found to supervene on three items, one of which is a property, Plato proves to be right after all.

If, contrary to Kant, a metaphysical proposition can be at once logically synthetic and epistemologically a posteriori in character, I believe I have shown how it can have an analytic a priori status as well. Witness the Principle of Identity, in defence of which, in chapter after chapter, I have undertaken to 'run a gauntlet' of dialectical objections reminiscent of Plato's insistence on such an imperative when it comes to metaphysical first principles. The trick here is to notice that, beginning with the

Fregean deduction of Herr Krug's pen in Chapter 4 and extending on to the Tarskian challenge of Chapter 5, *what* straight logic
is supposed to consist in is found to be much more problematic
than Kant was prepared to believe. These two sorts of metaphysical proposition being acknowledged, my readiness after ZF
to be hospitable to the synthetic a priori as a third variety
is almost mandated by purely taxonomic considerations. Merely
because non-Euclidean geometries that deny the parallels postulate have been shown to be logically consistent, does not entitle
one to conclude that Kant was mistaken in supposing that Euclid
provides us with the only viable geometry. If denying the parallels
postulate could be shown to issue in a contradiction, the postulate would have to be taken as analytic, and Kant *would* then be
refuted. On the positive side, Kant's 'proof' that being the shortest distance between two points is not logically entailed by the
concept 'straight line' has failed to satisfy those who are antecedently persuaded that the expression 'straight line' just means
the shortest distance between two points. Kant argues as follows:
'My concept *straight* contains nothing of quantity but only of
quality. The concept of the shortest is wholly an addition, and
cannot be derived through any process of analysis, from the
concept of the straight line. Intuition, therefore, must here be
called in; only by its aid is the synthesis possible.' Alluding to
Aristotle's categories of quality and quantity, Kant may be supposed to be considering all the lines that might be drawn between
any two points. Classified with respect to quality, there will then
be curved lines, looped lines, doubly looped lines, jagged lines,
everywhere non-differentiable lines, straight lines, and so on.
Classified with respect to quantity, the longest and the shortest
will interest us especially. The longest? There is no such thing.
Precisely, which is what I take to be Kant's point. If a 'glerb' is,
by definition, the longest distance between two points and a 'flit'
is the shortest, glerbs and flits will be conceptually on a par. Only
intuition can assure us of the non-existence of the one and the
uniqueness, as well as the straightness, of the other, and it is
through its means that a qualitative concept is synthesized with a
quantitative one.

Ironically, it is only after one has succeeded in some intuitive, or at least quasi-intuitive, fashion in envisaging what a non-Euclidean space might really be like that one is entitled to say farewell to Euclid. Einstein came to believe that a rocket fired straight up into the sky and keeping to a straight path throughout its flight—well, as straight a path as space affords—will eventually, after travelling a finite distance, come (so to speak) full circle, by returning to its point of origin. It was only to be expected that Einstein's conceit, which he proposed as a serious physical hypothesis, should come to be acknowledged as a logical possibility. A logical possibility? But that was Kant's position, and my lapse here indicates how very prone the professional philosopher is to go astray in this matter. Kant takes two straight lines enclosing a space to be both an absolutely impossible state of affairs and a logically possible one in the precise sense that no pair of contradictory propositions is entailed by it. For that is precisely what the synthetic a priori is all about, and the contemporary philosopher's befuddlement here, simply on the level of terminology, betrays his radical estrangement from the issue. There are other cases, however, where he turns out to be much more open to it than he realizes. Consider a four-dimensional super-cube that stands to a cube as a cube in its turn stands to a square. Mathematical theorems regarding it can be readily proved: for example, that the super-cube has 16 vertices in each of which 4 of the 32 straight edges meet, and that the super-cube is bounded by 8 proper cubes. Conceding that a super-cube made of wood, say, is almost certainly logically possible in the narrow sense, philosophers are very reluctant to admit that there really could be any such thing, and they are thus attracted to the suggestion that the statement 'There does not exist a wooden super-cube' yields a synthetic proposition that is known by us to be true on a priori grounds. At the same time they have been so intimidated by the eclipse of Euclid that they keep their reservations about the super-cube very much *in petto*.

This excursion into a fourth dimension of space provides a clue to an important argument of Kant, regarding incongruous counterparts, that scholars have often despaired of elucidating. Incongruous counterparts, as Paul Horwich writes, are 'objects such as a right hand and a left hand, of the same size and shape, that are mirror images of each other'. The right-angle triangles in Fig. 1 also qualify as such, for as long as one is merely allowed to slide them around in a plane, they can never be made to coincide. Availing oneself of the third dimension, one can of course flip over the one on the left so that it fits tight on the other. Analogously, if a right hand could be flipped over into a fourth dimension, it, too, could be brought to occupy the region vacated by the corresponding left hand. While logically possible, Kant rules out any such flipping on synthetic a priori grounds, thereby deriving the following contradiction regarding space as such: (1) if there are any two objects of the same size and shape, either can occupy the region vacated by the other, while (2) in the specific case of incongruous counterparts, that is quite impossible. Proving thus to be a 'transcendental illusion', space can no longer be taken to characterize things in themselves, and our sensory experience is rather like an Escher or Penrose drawing in which things are represented as being a certain way when that way is one in which things could never possibly be. How Kant can suppose that his own conclusion here is not properly metaphysical—namely, that being spatially extended can never pertain to anything whatever, at any rate in so far as it exists in itself—wiser heads than mine will have to explain. The absence in Kant of any thematic inquiry into precisely what it is for a thing to exist (or fail to exist) in itself one can only deplore.

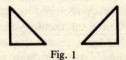

Fig. 1

Strikingly—and this was recognized at the time by more acute observers—the logical positivists, being empiricists of a fairly traditional variety, were found to be themselves committed in their own clandestine fashion to the synthetic a priori when they insisted, in effect, that to be is to be empirically verifiable. Take the proposition that there exists something that transcends all possible experience. That the proposition can be shown to harbour a logical inconsistency, no one (*pace* Berkeley) is seriously prepared to believe. Its denial, then, cannot be an analytic proposition. Synthetic, this negative proposition can only be known to be true on a priori grounds, and the positivist is thereby convicted of a *tu quoque*. The example is instructive more generally. Eschewing all commitment to the synthetic a priori turns out to be much more difficult than is commonly supposed, and one is thus well advised to keep a sharp look-out for its covert presence. Ready to hand in fact is the ZF intuition into the truth of the foundation axiom, on the strength of which one insists that 'the set of all doubtleton sets' fails in its effort to identify something; for, despite Russell's paradox, hypothesizing any such set is presumed to be free of outright inconsistency as a point of logic— which of course explains why the foundation axiom is needed. The proposition that there is no such set being thus confessed to be synthetic, it is in effect credited with having an a priori status as well. A surprising result? By no means. Appeals to intuition— let them be as breezily informal as you please—can hardly fail to smack of the synthetic a priori, and if the present generation of philosophers has lost sight of that elementary fact, earlier generations recognized it as a commonplace.

Although Kant must be credited with formulating it as an explicit challenge to the pretensions of metaphysics, the synthetic a priori was in fact anticipated by Leibniz when he distinguished his two fundamental principles of rationality—namely, the principle of non-contradiction and the principle of sufficient reason—for if the former suffices to ground the truths of mathematics, the latter is required to ground the truths of metaphysics, and of rational theology in particular. For the second principle insists on a reason (or cause or explanation) for everything whatsoever. In just about so many words, then, Leibniz assigns a synthetic a priori status to the principle of sufficient reason, readily conceding that one can deny it without fear of inconsistency. After Kant, when the synthetic a priori came to be scorned across the board as a pitiful refuge of obscurantism, the prospects of rational theology of necessity appeared very dim. Its last major manifestation was probably Husserl's phenomenology (sharply distinguished as a point of principle from classical ontology), which was explicitly designed to issue in synthetic a priori truths concerning the invariants of (different types of) intentional experience, but it is scarcely possible in all of Husserl's writings to find more than two or three casual examples of what such truths might look like. More serious still, despite extensive discussions of a methodological nature, one looks in vain for any effort on Husserl's part to allay the growing scepticism regarding the synthetic a priori as such, and it is thus scarcely surprising, bearing in mind the onslaught of the logical positivists, that Heidegger should choose, without so much as a by-your-leave, to drop this peculiarly vulnerable, yet surely indispensable, feature of the phenomenological programme. Sternly envisaged by Husserl as a rigorous science, phenomenology, on being stripped of the synthetic a priori, ends up in Sartre as a largely literary undertaking.

In its own dealings with the synthetic a priori during this whole period, the analytical school cannot be said to have acquitted itself with honour. An immense amount of ink was spent on such refractory cases as (1), and no more convincing example of a truth of Husserlian phenomenology can be given.

(1) Nothing is both red all over and green all over.

The consensus tended to be that (1) is known to be true on a priori grounds, and that since 'red' and 'green' admit of ostensive definition only, one could not expect to derive a contradiction from the denial of (1). So it was agreed then that (1) is a synthetic a priori truth? Not quite. It was decided to change the rules of the game. 'Analytic' was now redefined to cover more than merely logical truths in the narrow sense of the term. It was said that (1) is true merely by virtue of the meanings of the words 'red' and 'green', and since no one doubts that the meaning of a word is a matter of convention, (1) is then true by convention. Independently, logical truth *in* the narrow sense was urged to be itself a matter of convention, and thus the propriety of the innovation could appear altogether reasonable. As the mischief caused by these developments remains to this day, the jargon term 'analytic' has probably been ruined beyond repair.

Take the expression 'the meaning of the word "red"'. On the face of it, it appears to be a singular term that picks out an abstract entity. Beyond any mere convention, the truth of (1) would thus seem to proceed from the very nature of the two Platonic objects that answer to the words 'red' and 'green', though the Kantian, who is denied all access to these noumenal entities, cannot avail himself of them in defence of the synthetic a priori status of (1). One might also say, appealing now to a different abstract entity, that if the truth of the sentence (1) is doubtless to be explained at least in part by reference to certain conventions, the truth of the proposition expressed by (1) must be understood in very different terms.

The mischief caused by the analysts can be traced back to Kant himself, when he said that 'through analytic judgements our knowledge is not in any way extended', for they merely supply us with an 'explanation or elucidation of what has already been thought in our concepts, though in a confused manner'. No wonder Frege was persuaded that success in proving the truths of arithmetic to be analytic could not but 'suffice to put an end to the widespread contempt for analytic judgements and to the legend of the sterility of pure logic', as he writes at the end of Section 17 of the *Foundations of Arithmetic*. He was not to know that at the end of his life, having been seduced by Wittgenstein, Bertrand Russell could write, 'I fear that, to a mind of sufficient intellectual power, the whole of mathematics would appear trivial, as trivial as the statement that a four-legged animal is four-legged.' Like Kant before him, Russell is here conflating epistemic with logical considerations. Not merely logically analytic, 'All four-legged animals are four-legged' may be said to be epistemically (or doxastically) analytic as well, for no one, however stupid, could possibly believe something to be a four-legged animal without (also) believing it was four-legged. This is no mere matter of contingent empirical psychology, but an (analytic? synthetic?) a priori truth in its own right. It is easy now to show that not all logically analytic propositions of the form 'Every F is a G' are epistemically analytic, even for God. In fact, any statement that is epistemically synthetic for us is equally so for God. The question is always, whether someone (and here it is the stupid who are privileged) could possibly believe something to be an F without believing it to be a G. All the relevant mathematical cases will thus be at once logically analytic and epistemically synthetic, and it can therefore be insisted that in these cases epistemic synthesis takes place in the mind of God. That these cases, even so, might be expected to 'appear trivial' to him, can be of interest only to one engaged in trans-human psychology.

In a polemical vein, I have been assuming with Russell that the truths of arithmetic are characteristically analytic, though Russell himself knew better, thanks to his own paradox that refuted Frege's project. Even waiving the paradox, however, we have seen how Frege was required from the outset to presuppose the existence of sets in his consequently vain effort to establish the analyticity of arithmetic. Although almost all philosophers today probably believe in their bones that the propositions of arithmetic must be analytic, it has to be said that the technical results which have accumulated since Frege tend rather to support Kant in his conviction that they have a synthetic a priori status. Assume, indeed, that we know to be true propositions of the form 'There are exactly x prime numbers between y and z', and synthetic a priori truths about Platonic objects are delivered to us on a silver platter.

How the synthetic a priori can be found to underlie some of the more important metaphysical discussions of recent years, I propose to show in later chapters, beginning with the next.

19

Artificial Intelligence

Deliciously ambiguous, the expression 'artificial intelligence' may be taken in either of two ways, as being on a par with 'artificial pearls', where it is of course understood that artificial pearls are not pearls, or as being on a par with 'artificial light', where it is not to be doubted that artificial light is truly light. In general, an artificial F will or will not be an F, depending on the value of F. Coined by Marvin Minsky, the expression 'artificial intelligence' could be taken in his idiolect only as being on a par with 'artificial light'; though I am quite prepared to believe that, as one of the founders of the artificial intelligence enterprise, he was guileful enough to realize that if the term was to enter our common language as a neutral piece of nomenclature designating a whole new field of research, the greater the ambiguity of the term the better. One is thus invited to recall what Francis Bacon said of 'alloy in coin of gold and silver', that even while 'it embaseth it', it serves to 'make the metal work the better'.

The question of whether a purely physical account of the universe can accommodate mind surfaced for the first time in these pages in Chapter 17, where the more general issue of emergent entities had to be confronted in order to understand sets. Of still keener relevance to the volume as a whole is the following consideration. In accord with Aristotle, the metaphysician was seen at the outset of his inquiry to adopt as a working hypothesis, pending evidence to the contrary, the suggestion that our most authoritative understanding of reality is to be found in physics. His reflections on that hypothesis are thus to be styled precisely as meta-physics, and it is not long before, so engaged, he encounters the issue of mind. That approach to the question of mind fails, however, to capture the more specific flavour of my own undertaking, which engages physics very much at a remove, as mediated by mathematics. An intransigent materialist as a point of principle, Minsky is even more fundamentally a mathematician; and one is struck above all by how very far removed from the physical sciences is the anomalous field of artificial intelligence. No experiments are performed in anything like the fashion in which they are undertaken in the natural sciences, by way of verifying or falsifying hypotheses framed for the purpose of uncovering hitherto unknown laws of nature. Nor is the physical process of thinking (as we may suppose it to be) investigated by way of an examination of what goes on in a human being's brain when he is engaged in thinking. Any such inquiry is thought to bypass the essence of thinking, which is assumed to be an activity in which even robots may participate. Rather as the mathematician investigates circularity as such in abstraction from the bronze or wax in which it is realized on this or that occasion, so the researcher in artificial intelligence may address himself to thinking—that is, the exercise of intelligence—in perfect indifference as to whether it is realized in organic or inorganic materials, not to mention ectoplasm. So understood, thinking is seen to invite a mode of research that is more akin to mathematics than physics, and Minsky's professional expertise is thus found to be peculiarly suited to the endeavour. It is hardly an accident, then, that his (and Seymour Papert's) critique of Rosenblatt's perceptron should be subtitled 'An Introduction to Computational Geometry'. Designed for pattern recognition, but characterized in entirely abstract terms, the perceptron undertakes to 'compute' the global features of a figure on the basis of local information derived from scanning it bit by bit; and one theorem of the 'geometry' consists of the negative verdict that any such 'diameter-limited' device as Rosenblatt's is quite incapable of determining 'whether or not all the parts of any geometric figure are connected to one another'. Exploiting the ambiguity of 'artificial intelligence', one sort of researcher is admittedly content merely to *simulate* intelligent behaviour in his robots—call this 'soft AI'—while the other sort, to which Minsky belongs, being committed to 'hard AI', is ambitious enough to undertake to build machines that engage in thinking properly so-called. Invested with artificial intelligence, any such machine may be expected to be endowed with artificial life as well, though I believe it to be in the spirit of hard AI to be prepared to concede that, in sharp contrast with intelligence, 'life' is being predicated here only in the *alienans* mode in which one speaks of artificial pearls. A fine point, perhaps, but one has the sense that life is much more involved in matter than mind is; and one thus supposes that a person who, having died, perseveres into an afterlife as a disembodied spirit may continue thinking long after he has ceased to be alive. If any such 'spiritualistic' considerations should be felt to be alien to AI, one can only recall an astute remark of Hilary Putnam, that when one says, glibly enough, that the human brain is 'no more than a Turing machine', one is apt to forget—so abstract are these notions of a Turing machine or a Rosenblatt perceptron—that a disembodied spirit is quite capable of being either.

Suppose now the optimum case. A robot has been built that in all relevant respects exhibits the full range of 'adaptive behaviour' that one encounters in the most intelligent (and well-adjusted) human being. Ought the robot to be credited with the exercise of mind? Although the behaviourist, who is persuaded that mind is merely 'a certain function from sensory input to motor output', will readily answer in the affirmative, the proponent of hard AI need not be so easily satisfied. One wants to look into the 'black box' before rendering a verdict. Suppose further, then, that the computational geometry of Minsky and Papert has proceeded step by step from the 'construction' of such simple devices as the perceptron to that of the most versatile sort of abstract robot. Looking into the physical robot, they find not the miniaturized electronic circuitry that might well be felt to be dauntingly 'inscrutable', but a complex array of wheels, gears, and pulleys that enables them in the most perspicuous fashion to read into them—an exercise in hermeneutics—all the abstract devices that have been antecedently 'constructed' on the level of pure theory. *Now*, shall the robot be certified as a thinking thing? Suspending judgement on the issue, I am content here to explore what, without fear of hyperbole, one is entitled to call the metaphysics of hard AI. More narrowly still, I am addressing the logico-epistemic status of universal propositions having the form both of (a): 'Every robot realizing such and such abstract specifications is a thing engaged in thinking about . . .' and of (b): 'Everything whose purely physical description consists in . . . is a thing engaged in thinking about . . .'. If the underlying principle of hard A I is correct, there are true propositions of the (b) as well as (a) type that are found to enjoy a synthetic a priori status.

This link between hard A I and the synthetic a priori may be somewhat disorientating, if only for the reason that one tends to associate hard A I with tough-minded philosophers, the synthetic a priori with the tender-minded variety. One is thus being called on to reallocate whole blocks of one's thinking from one part of the brain to another—so, at any rate, I dare hypothesize—when one is asked to associate hard A I with the synthetic a priori. The basic thought, however, is simple enough. When it is asserted that (this robot or) any robot with such and such abstract specifications is engaged in thinking, it is not to be supposed that an analytic proposition is being advanced, as if one who rejects hard A I could be convicted ultimately of an outright contradiction. But it is worth noting in this regard that the computational geometry of Minsky and Papert does consist entirely of analytic truths! Defining the (relevant class of) perceptron in precise terms, one then deduces its incapacity simply on the basis of local reports to compute the global connectedness of Fig. 2 by way of contrast with the global disconnectedness of Fig. 3; and since 'the presently identified functions of receptor cells are all diameter-limited . . . an animal will require more than neurosynaptic "summation" effects to make these cells compute connectedness', for 'only the most advanced animals can apprehend this complicated visual concept'.[1] Logically analytic, the truths of computational geometry are epistemically synthetic; accordingly, there is no excuse for philosophers continuing to depreciate logically analytic propositions as being less than fully informative. It is not such analytic propositions, however, but the logically synthetic ones of hard A I, to which our attention is being directed principally, and one must then ask if these propositions of both the (a) and the (b) varieties are to be assigned an a posteriori status, which would at least render them unproblematical.

---

[1] Marvin Minsky and Seymour Papert, *Perceptrons* (Cambridge, Mass.: MIT Press, 1969), p. 14.

The difficulty here turns on the fact that from the outset AI never aspired to be a *natural* science, and its propositions, with the form 'Thinking consists in . . .' or 'Intelligence consists in . . .' (anticipated by Hobbes in his maxim 'Ratiocination is computation'), were not expected to be verified through an inspection of brain processes. But such an aposterioristic approach does remain available to AI, and we may distinguish empirical AI from pure AI, where it is only the latter that involves the synthetic a priori. Too 'solipsistic', propositions of both the (a) and the (b) varieties entail that a robot might be engaged in thinking even in the absence of any environment whatever; accordingly, these propositions must be enriched to include (abstract and physical) descriptions of diverse environments, which, if recent discussions are to be trusted, may be expected to determine the very content of our robot's thinking in fairly deep ways as it interacts now with this, now with that one.

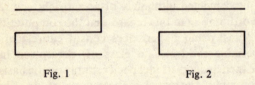

Fig. 1   Fig. 2

As to precisely how a priori synthesis is to be negotiated between the physicalistic and the mentalistic concepts featured in any enriched proposition of type (b), Kant is inevitably instructive with his appeal to intuition. In a more graphic vein, we may characterize pure AI as involving a kinematic/cinematic approach. The kinematics is twofold. First, there are the movements of the robot as it interacts with the bodies in its environment; call this the behavioural dimension. Second, there are the movements of the bodies within the robot as *they* interact with one another; call this the computational dimension. Both these scenarios, the one external, the other internal, are now to be viewed cinematically, and I am here referring literally to a motion picture that undertakes to display mind at work. Not that there is any need for the motion picture to be a re-enactment of episodes that have actually taken place. It is not like a film that shows the decomposition of water into hydrogen and oxygen. Such a film can provide knowledge of water's constitution only if one is assured that the film is veridical. In sharp contrast, AI cinematics may be entirely fictional, even while allowing us to read off from them true propositions of the (b) variety, thereby confirming their aprioristic, intuitional character. No single roll of film will of course suffice to enable us to derive a proposition belonging to this hermeneutic phenomenology of mind. Recalling Ryle's dispositional account of mind, touched on in Chapter 7, we shall need infinitely many rolls of film, simply in order to unpack a single low-level proposition of type (b), for (sticking to the external scenario) we shall have to envisage all the relevant counterfactuals, each assigned film of its own, that are required as underpinning for such a simple event as a robot's raising its hand in warning. Easier by far is actually building the robot! It is not to be supposed, however, that this entry by default into the a posteriori, where sense perception and not merely the 'transcendental imagination' is called upon, has any essential role to play when it comes to pure AI. Building an actual robot merely projects into reality the aprioristic content antecedently entertained by transcendental cinematics. The point is to *construct* the robot, no matter whether it be in reality or merely in the imagination.

The metaphysics of pure AI is ultimately found to consist in the conviction that mind supervenes on matter by way of a synthetic a priori link of the one to the other.

20

Essence

Is being a horse an essential property of every horse? Can we so much as conceive the abstract possibility of a horse's ceasing to be a horse even while continuing to exist? One would suppose not, and one is thus readily perplexed by what anti-essentialists may be up to when they persist in denying the obvious. For it is not only horses, but swallows as well, that have the essential property of being in the one case a horse and in the other a swallow. And the same holds *mutatis mutandis* even for mice, not to mention bees, spiders, worms, beetles, caterpillars, eels, newts, lizards, chameleons, and the rest. 'But surely this accumulation of examples is quite unnecessary, as the single instance of the horse suffices of itself to prove the point,' someone might say. Not so. If there is no need to extend the list, it is only because one subversive item on it is already ready to hand, inviting the anti-essentialist to press his attack against what he can only deplore as the massively stereotypical thinking to which the Aristotelian in his smugness is addicted. As if, like Adam in the Garden of Eden, one had only to observe a horse or a group of horses in order not merely to abstract from them the universal 'horse', but to recognize it as being an essential feature of such creatures. Pre-lapsarian innocence indeed!

An essentialist like David Wiggins would probably reply as follows: 'Even if a horse were (as you propose) to undergo metamorphosis into an elephant or at any rate into something indistinguishable, on the micro as well as the macro level, from a bona fide elephant, it would still be a horse, for one must distinguish between mere phase sortals like "tadpole" and "caterpillar" or even "First Lord of the Admiralty", which apply to a creature only during a phase of its existence, and proper sortals like "horse" or "man", which cover its career from start to finish.' A mere verbal point, surely, for if we now ask what it is precisely that a horse is committed to being throughout its career, what else can be said but this: such as to have the word 'horse' apply to it, where that has no independent content of its own. In a more substantive vein Wiggins might argue as follows: 'If our biological theories are correct (and it would be impertinent of you to indulge in captious reservations on this point), the metamorphosis you project is simply ruled out as being contrary to the nature of things.' No doubt, but after Hume, the status of a law of nature—and here one must turn from the secondary terrain of biology to the primary terrain of physics—has been rendered very problematical. The classic case remains that of causation, which is all the more relevant when, recalling the opening paragraph of Chapter 2, one realizes that if in the one case we are concerned with a property belonging to a thing in no merely accidental fashion but as a matter of necessity, then, in the other, it is not enough for one sort of event to follow another merely by accident, let it be as often and as exceptionlessly as you please, for a causal relation to obtain between them. More is required, and that more does seem to be that the later sort of event follow upon the earlier one precisely as a matter of compulsion or necessity. The trouble here, as Hume emphasized, is that the only handle on necessity available to us has to do with the 'relations of ideas', as when we insist that 9 is necessarily odd by virtue of a conceptual link between the notions '9' and 'odd'. Or when, recalling Chapter 1, we say both that being a mathematician necessarily involves being rational and that being a bicyclist necessarily involves being two-legged, leaving entirely open whether 'this concrete individual' who is both mathematician and bicyclist is or is not necessarily rational or necessarily two-legged. If tough-minded Humeans have characteristically identified necessity with analyticity, the more tender-minded Kantians have allowed for a synthetic a priori kind of necessity as well. Notice, however, that their rival accounts of necessity, the one stringent, the other generous, have one decisive feature in common: necessity is bound up with the a priori. It is, however, an a posteriori sort of necessity—a necessity in the things themselves—that is called on when it comes to essence and causation. It is thus no wonder that neither the one nor the other, neither causation nor essence, has any role to play in Quine's universe. As a point of scholarship, one knew of course that a posteriori necessity was central to Aristotle's thinking, notably in the last chapter of his *Posterior Analytics*; but the modern philosopher could only avert his eyes from the doctrine in acute embarrassment, feeling quite incapable of finding a proper slot for it in his epistemological scheme. Much as he might scorn the synthetic a priori, he never doubted that here at least was a doctrine to be refuted. Aristotle's doctrine, by contrast, was simply beyond the pale of polite discourse.

In January 1970 Saul Kripke gave his three trail-blazing lectures on 'Naming and Necessity' at Princeton University, and, really for the first time since the late seventeenth century, when John Locke's critique of it was beginning to sweep through Europe, the whole issue of Aristotelian essentialism was instantly reopened precisely on the strength of Kripke's insistence that necessity could be pried loose from the a priori. It is not to be supposed, however, that the logical approach to metaphysics that defines my project must now yield to an epistemic orientation, granted that the distinction between a priori and a posteriori must be allowed to be the special preserve of epistemology. How it is logic, not epistemology, that takes pride of place in the Kripkean renewal of essentialism comes out vividly enough against the specifically Quinean background of the issue. For it was a puzzle in logic proper, formulated by Quine, that led to a whole flurry of activity to resolve it, only one of which proved to involve a return to essentialism. More even than the puzzle itself, it was Quine's proposed solution that led to the keenest anxiety, notably in the ranks of his own more mathematically minded students. Quine simply had to be wrong! That was the universal reaction, though one was disconcerted to find oneself almost totally at a loss when it came to specifying exactly how he went wrong.

Breath-takingly audacious, with the kind of inspired lunacy reserved to the great philosopher, Quine was prepared to argue that one was mistaken if one supposed that 9 was essentially or necessarily odd. Even Locke would have been nonplussed, and we can imagine him protesting, 'My anti-essentialism was never intended to be so thoroughgoing as to apply to mind-independent objects like 9, presumed to exist outside space and time as Platonic entities. Let the existence of 9 be granted, and I do not doubt that oddness belongs to it essentially. By contrast, pick at random some time-bound, concrete object available to sense perception—say, a bicyclist. My point, of course, was merely to show why an analytic proposition like "(x) x is a bicyclist $\supset$ x is two-legged" fails to certify the concrete individual as being essentially two-legged.' One must not expect to find the kind of clarity that Locke is here bringing to the issue in the literature of the time. So devitalized and decadent was pre-Kripkean anti-essentialism, which lived mindlessly off its Lockean inheritance, that even so distinguished a professional philosopher of the era as C. I. Lewis could write, 'Traditionally any attribute required for the application of a term'—and here the terms 'bicyclist' and 'mathematician' serve as our stock-in-trade—'is said to be of the essence of the thing named. It is, of course, meaningless to speak of the essence of a thing except relative to its being named by a particular term.' Is it being suggested, then, that every attribute of a thing, when the thing is taken in itself, absolutely speaking, apart from 'being named by a particular term', is really only accidental to it? An intriguing thought, certainly, and we may thus distinguish two sorts of anti-essentialism: (a) the variety that we are here considering, which we may denominate 'accidentalism', and (b) relativistic anti-essentialism, of the sort examined in Chapter 2.

Less than entirely novel, Quine's puzzle of the planets goes as follows: (1) 9 = the number of planets; (2) the number of planets could have been even (if Mars, say, had exploded a thousand years ago). Recalling Leibniz's law from Chapter 10, we now conclude that (3) 9 could have been even, and hence that 9 is not necessarily or essentially odd. In the same vein we can also argue that since (4) 9 *is* necessarily odd, it follows, from (4) and (3), that (5) 9 both is and is not necessarily odd.

So do we have here a recapitulation of Quine's paradox of the mathematical bicyclist? Not quite. Witty enough as an eloquent expression of familiar anti-essentialist sentiments, the one paradox has nothing original to contribute to the philosophical debate. The startling originality of the other lies in Quine's readiness to apply a familiar enough strategy to such an unexpected context as that of abstract entities, with the outcome that a certain object, taken quite by itself, is to be regarded without fear of inconsistency as being both (*a*) necessarily odd and (*b*) not necessarily odd, seeing that those characteristics are merely elliptical for, respectively, (*c*) necessarily odd *qua* being the sum of 1 and 1 and 1 . . ., and (*d*) not necessarily odd *qua* numbering how many planets the sun possesses.

Too idiosyncratic, the paradox of the planets fails to convey the extent to which the Quine–Kripke quarrel over essentialism was grounded in antecedent controversy over (the scope of) logic itself; so much so that, as in the case of our neo-Meinongians in Chapter 11, one can even suspect that the metaphysics comes into play only secondarily, providing a rationale for specifically logical considerations. In the present instance it is the reputability of modal logic, which can be traced all the way back to Aristotle, that is the *casus belli*. Assuming a virtual dictatorship over the new logic in the forties, Quine will be recalled as having purged it of set theory with *its* metaphysics. But that was only one move. Almost equally fateful was his veto of modal logic, as being vitiated by tacit involvement in Aristotelian essentialism. Thus Plato and Aristotle both come into play *vis-à-vis* the new logic, and it is precisely this moment, when the clarification of logic affords the primary desideratum, that inaugurates the full-scale renewal of classical metaphysics in our era. If the presence of Aristotelian as well as Platonic elements in Frege's thinking have independently engaged much of my attention, it is the combination of the two, Frege and Quine, that lies at the core of my synoptic programme. 'Much as we may dislike Aristotelian essentialism as philosophers,' goes a subversive thought of the fifties that was perhaps never fully articulated, 'we are logicians first, and if the only way that we can keep our modal logic is by relinquishing our anti-essentialism, well, one pays one's money and one takes one's choice.'

At the very least the machinery of modal logic helps to clarify such questions as 'Is every horse (caterpillar) necessarily a horse (caterpillar)?' and 'Is (everything that is identical with) the number of planets necessarily odd?' For as Thomas Aquinas observed in the Middle Ages, even the trivial question 'Is every white wall necessarily white?' admits of being glossed in two diverse ways, either *de dicto* or *de re*.

(1) (x) x is white $\cdot$ x is a wall $\supset$ x is white.

(2) $\Box$ (x) x is white $\cdot$ x is a wall $\supset$ x is white.

(3) (x) x is white $\cdot$ x is a wall $\supset$ $\Box$ x is white.

(4) (x) x numbers how many planets Sol has $\supset$ x is odd.

(5) (x) x numbers how many planets Sol has $\supset$ x is odd.

(6) (x) x numbers how many planets Sol has $\supset$ $\Box$ x is odd.

(7) $\sim \Box$ (x) x numbers how many planets Sol has $\supset$ $\Box$ x is odd.

Thanks to (1) being not only true, but necessarily (even analytically) true, (2), which is to be read as 'Necessarily (1)' or 'It is necessarily the case that (1)', is also true. Aquinas's question, then, requires an affirmative answer when it is taken *de dicto*—that is to say, in respect to the dictum or proposition associated with it, namely, (1). But there is also a *de re* reading of the question, which invites us to consider any white wall and ask of it—namely, the very *res*, or thing, itself—whether being white is so essential—that is, necessary—to it that even God could not arrange for the thing to exist as black or red. (3) must then be false, for it says that if something is a white wall, it is necessarily white in the emphatic sense that its very existence is inescapably bound up with its being so.

More interesting are (4), (5), and (6). Although (4) is true, it is only contingently so, since there are many possible worlds in which it is false. Accordingly, (5) is false, but (6) is true, though only contingently so! None the less, the merely contingent truth of (6) suffices to assure us that the thing which happens to number how many planets there are—namely, 9—is necessarily or essentially odd, for in no possible state of affairs is that thing even. Take some possible world in which (6) is false. In that world the thing that numbers how many planets there are might well be 8. Consider now someone who does not know whether (6) or (4) is true. He can be expected to know, however, that *if* (4) is true, then so is (6). Especially revealing is the mix of *de dicto* and *de re* modality in (6), for it features *de re* necessity and *de dicto* contingency, in consequence of which (7) is true.

Still riveted by the truth of (6) and the vindication of essentialism that it entails, there remains only our bemusement over having been coaxed into saying, 'The number of planets could have been even' when that very number, 9, could not possibly be so ever. It is here that Kripke's distinction between a rigid and a non-rigid designator saves the day. How explain our readiness to allow both that (1) Benjamin Franklin might well have been the first president of the USA if (say) Washington had been killed in the Revolutionary War and that (2) the first president of the USA was Washington, even though we recoil from the suggestion that (3) Franklin might have been Washington in certain counterfactual circumstances? Presumably, Franklin has the essential property of not being (identical with) Washington! Co-referential singular terms, the proper name 'Washington', and the definite description 'the first president of the USA' evidently operate very differently in modal contexts. Although 'the *F*' does pick out Washington in the non-modal context of (2), it fails to do so in the modal context of (1). Being rigid designators, proper names stick to their referents in all possible worlds, whereas definite descriptions, being non-rigid designators, pick out different items in different worlds.

Even waiving the issue of essentialism, systematic modal thinking cannot be said to be an activity in which, historically, the modern philosopher has excelled. Especially noteworthy is Frege's lack of modal sophistication when it comes to his deduction of Herr Krug's pen from the Principle of Identity. Recalling the derivation from Chapter 4, we have only to ask whether there is a possible world in which the premiss is true and the conclusion false, in order to satisfy ourselves today that the argument cannot be valid *sans phrase*, though we are free to provide a niche for it in our logic as being F-valid, or Frege-valid. It is this 'possible worlds' approach to validity, even as regards non-modal logic, and not the misgivings of our neo-Meinongians that explains my uneasiness with regard to the deduction of Herr Krug's pen. Not that Frege is quite without a reply. 'So on your view', he can be heard to protest, 'the following is a valid argument: "It is (not) raining. Therefore, there is at least one possible world.'' For you cannot expect me to concede that there is a possible world where the premiss is true and the conclusion is false.'

Today the standard reply to *that* goes as follows. A convenient device for thinking about validity, the notion of a possible world need not be taken with so much ontological seriousness when it comes merely to rejecting such arguments as the deduction of Herr Krug's pen. And the further rejoinder to this is beautifully summed up by Quine in a single word: 'double-talk'. As if one simply had the right to help oneself to an abstract entity, for possible worlds *are* abstract entities (*pace* David Lewis), and at the same time to foreswear all ontological commitment to it. Although one can, of course, earn that right by showing how ostensible reference to the objectionable item can be paraphrased away in some more or less periphrastic fashion, it is not to be supposed that the prospects of success in this particular case are very bright. My ontological or onto-logical argument for the existence of possible worlds and *a fortiori* abstract entities—the appeal to rain is only perfunctory—must not be dismissed as frivolous, for it merely encapsulates the familiar view that logic as such is committed to possible worlds. Arguably, then, Frege is right. There *are* logical objects—not sets, however, but possible worlds. On the way to first principles, the logical approach to metaphysics might even be expected to discover them ultimately in the foundations of logic itself; thus my protracted engagement with the Principle of Identity in earlier chapters may be viewed as all of a piece with what I am doing here.

If the traditional philosopher has typically regarded abstract entities as mere *entia rationis*, one can only relish Plato's peals of laughter in the background, as if those entities of reason upon which the philosopher relies could fail to be real! As the patrimony of the logician, possible worlds serve to vindicate not only Plato but Aristotle's essentialism as well. For the essential properties of Socrates prove to be precisely those that preserve his very identity in every possible world from which he is not absent. A more secure grip on specifically modal thinking would have saved the modern philosopher from supposing that there can be no a posteriori necessity. Take the argument '$(\exists x)\ x$ = Herr

Krug's pen, therefore ◊ (∃x) x = Herr Krug's pen', whose validity is certified by the age-old metaphysical principle 'Actuality entails possibility'. Because any proposition of the form '◊p' is acknowledged to be necessarily true if true at all, the conclusion of our argument, namely that it is possible that something is identical with Herr Krug's pen, must be a necessary truth. Yet it is not the case that someone who has never heard of either Herr Krug or his pen could come to know that truth on an a priori basis.

Even Quine will accept the argument. For his rejection of modal logic extends only to *de re* modality, not to the *de dicto* variety. As long as □ and ◊ serve merely as external operators, as in (2) and (5), they are free of essentialist commitments. Very different is their internal use, as in (3) and (6), where one is to be convicted of 'quantifying into a modal context'. Not that the purely external use of modal operators commands Quine's full approbation. Having already established in non-modal logic that 'p x ~p' is a valid statement form, one is engaged in the merest window-dressing on his view when one adopts a modal notation in order to write '□ (p x ~p)'.

21

No Entity without Identity

'There is no question in philosophy more abstruse', writes Hume, 'than that concerning the identity . . . of . . . a person,' and he does not hesitate to add that 'we must have recourse to the most profound metaphysics to give a satisfactory answer to it'. It is not personal identity in particular, however, but identity as such that calls for this profound metaphysics; and if one's very life depended on successfully summing up in four words the underlying rationale of the new essentialism, one could only be urged to reply, free of all fear, '*No* entity without identity'. That the slogan has been patented by Quine to serve his own ends, among which his anti-essentialism is not negligible, undermines the reply not at all. Nor is it to be thought that the maxim must be glossed in some fairly deviant fashion if the essentialist is to pre-empt it for his own purpose, which is precisely to see Quine hoist on his own petard. Devised in effect by Frege, the maxim is tacitly invoked by Wittgenstein at a key point in his famous private language argument, and if it is only Quine who expressly celebrates it as normative for the whole enterprise of ontology, Kripke is to be credited with pressing its modal version, 'No entity without trans-world identity'. Invoking these august names of analytical philosophy, we can safely say that the maxim expresses the fundamental principle of being as such, or being *qua* being, as regards the entire movement.

How the maxim is to be applied *in concreto* we have noticed twice already, once with reference to functions at the end of Chapter 9 and once, but more vividly, with regard to meanings, at the end of Chapter 11, where it was found to operate in tandem with Quine's *other* slogan, 'Explication is elimination'. A formidable combination! One can be sure that such an object lesson is more to be prized than any defence of these principles on the level of high generality. Arguably even more vivid, if inevitably more enigmatic, is Wittgenstein's 'No entity without identity' in connection with the following experiment designed to show that 'an "inner process" stands in need of outward criteria'. Press your thumb into your cheek. Call the sensation 'S' and relish it as a pure phenomenological datum. Now press your thumb into your neck. Is that sensation also S? Well, if 'S' is the name of a sensation-token, as a newcomer to the topic might be pardoned for supposing, the answer must surely be no. But the context of the question being supplied by Wittgenstein's classic discussion, *we* know that 'S' was assigned to the sort or type of sensation that was produced in your cheek by your thumb. But does the definite description encapsulated in the last fifteen words of the previous sentence really succeed in denoting something? Is the animal in the boughs of that tree the same (sort of) animal as the one that lies purring here on the rug? Well, both are cats, but this is a Siamese cat. So there is more than one *sort* to be considered. In the one case as in the other, there can be no *re*-identification of an object, seeing that, context aside, no object was properly identified in the first place. Which I take to be precisely Frege's original point. *What* object has been identified on some occasion can only be elucidated by envisaging the criteria for its re-identification on some other occasion.

Section 62 of Frege's *The Foundations of Arithmetic* being the canonical text, we find there the thought that 'the number of F's' can pick out an object only if we have in hand a criterion enabling us to decide whether 'the number of G's' picks out the same or a different one. Generalizing, Frege writes, 'If we are to use the symbol *a* to signify an object, we must have a criterion for deciding in all cases whether *b* is the same as *a* even if it is not always in our power to apply this criterion.' One such object, Frege's favourite example, is the direction of a certain line, which can be shown to be identical with the direction of a different line merely by showing that the lines are parallel. Different lines but same direction, hence same object, with parallelism serving as the criterion of identity not of lines but of their direction.

Heraclitus' paradox now admits of a deft solution, following a proposal of David Wiggins. One *can* step into the same river twice, but in doing so, one must not expect to step into the same water. Nor in re-identifying the river on a later occasion will one be re-identifying the same water. So the river cannot be identical with the water. At any instant, then, two coincident objects need to be distinguished: the river and the water of which it is composed. Accordingly, two material objects are found to occupy the same place at the same time, something one would previously have thought impossible. Mere observation can never suffice to enable one to pick out a Fregean object; a concept is always required to mediate the process. For it can always be asked, 'Are you drawing my attention to the table or to the (quantity of) wood that composes it?' Typically found in a dispersed or scattered form, these quantities of wood, water, and so forth may now enter one's ontology as proper objects under the auspices of 'No entity without identity'.

Employed by Wittgenstein in order to undermine irreducibly private objects, the principle is no less destructively used by Quine against properties, which are to be replaced by sets. Here again a concrete case hits close to home. Is (the property of) being self-identical identical with (the property of) existing? Although the ontological enterprise as such was found to have a rich stake in an affirmative answer, I can hardly be said to have shown that a single object is being picked out here by different linguistic items. And this is the easy case! For (*pace* our neo-Meinongians) the 'two' properties are doxastically as well as logically equivalent, and Quine's critique of properties is widely thought to acquire its bite only in the case of logically equivalent but doxastically non-equivalent properties. The point is most vividly put in connection with propositions, which are also 'eliminated' by Quine. If logically equivalent propositions are identical—and that is conceded to be the most foolproof criterion on the market—then there is only one logically necessary truth, since all such propositions are true in all possible worlds. Where an answer to Quine's challenge is typically sought—namely, in a doxastic criterion—I have already indicated; but that is almost too gratifying when it comes to my own project of glossing the word 'existence' in terms of self-identity. No matter. The central point here is that, in the controversy over properties and propositions, 'No entity without identity' is accepted as normative by all parties. As regards the sentences (a) '2 + 2 = 4', (b) 'There is no greatest prime number,' and (c) '5 + 7 = 12', no one is prepared to allow that God is entitled to rule, apart from any general criterion and relying solely on case-by-case intuition, that while (a) and (b) happen to express the same proposition (c) happens to express a different one. Designed above all to block any such theological conceit, 'No entity without identity' is not to be glossed as saying merely that $(1)(x)x = x$ or even that $(2)(x)(y)x = y \times \sim (x = y)$.

No more beautiful use of the principle can be found than in Quine's recent, scarcely noticed conversion to the ZF conception of sets when he observes that 'ungrounded classes have an individuation problem'. One has only to consider 'the celebrated principle of the individuation of classes, namely that they are identical if and only if their members are identical'. Sets are thus individuated 'only insofar as their members are already'— antecedently—'individuated, and on this score an ungrounded class totters over an infinite regress'.[1] Much deeper than my own effort to 'ground' the ZF conception of a set in the ontology of emergence proves to be Quine's grounding it in the still more fundamental maxim 'No entity without identity', though in both cases the metaphysician is seen to be striking back at the mathematician.

How the principle bears on the new essentialism can be brought out trenchantly enough in connection with Kripke's doctrine concerning 'the necessity of origins'. Entering his workshop with the aim of making a reproduction of a Chippendale table, a carpenter has to decide which of two indistinguishable blocks of wood to use, C or D. Tossing a coin which lands heads, he makes his table out of C. He can later be heard to say, 'If the coin had landed tails, this table', striking it with his fist, 'would have been made out of D not C.' A natural enough thought, but one that Kripke convicts of a profound metaphysical mistake. The carpenter's contrary-to-fact conditional can only be evaluated after we have consulted the possible world in which the coin lands tails. Although in that world (call it W_2 to distinguish it from W_1, the actual world) it is indeed D and not C out of which the carpenter

---

[1] L. E. Hahn and P. A. Schilpp, eds., *The Philosophy of W. V. Quine* (La Salle, Ill.: Open Court, 1986), p. 590.

makes *a* table, is it precisely this table—call it 'A'—that is made there? In order to help us track A from one possible world to another, consider now W_3, in which the carpenter, instead of tossing his coin, is so enticed by the fine grain of both C and D that he takes on the burden of making two tables, more or less simultaneously. If in W_3 A can only be supposed to be the table made out of C, surely it must be the other table made in W_3—call it 'B'—that is produced in W_2. For it is scarcely to be imagined that there is a W_4 in which the carpenter makes A out of D and B out of C. It is not as if there were something the carpenter did in W_1 that resulted in his making A rather than B out of C; nor is there even a law of nature (as that term is used in the philosophy of science) whose contravention by a divine miracle might have issued on that occasion in B being fashioned out of C.

If my accumulation of circumstantial detail is felt to be excessive to the point of redundancy, it should be borne in mind that vividness is at a premium here where Kripke is engaged in activating our modal intuitions into a diversified sheaf of possible worlds. The operative notion is indeed that of intuition in a fairly Kantian sense, as one finds oneself peering long and hard into these almost cinematic displays in one's effort to decide whether an object in one world is or is not identical with one in another. We are thus tempted not at all to share Nathan Salmon's suspicion that a metaphysical rabbit is being pulled out of a linguistic hat, though linguistic considerations do have their negative part to play in knocking the scales from our eyes. For our carpenter might have been content to say, 'If the coin had landed tails, the table I made yesterday would have been fashioned out of D not C', where 'the *F*' serves merely as a non-rigid designator, thereby allowing us to assent to *this* counterfactual.

If only as a rule of thumb, the mere mention of the word 'intuition' in philosophy can never be allowed to go unaccompanied by at least a nod in the direction of the synthetic a priori, and even apart from any such general heuristic, there is a more immediate consideration that alerts us to its presence. In the course of defending his doctrine regarding the necessity of origins and with specific reference to his table, Kripke writes that the doctrine is 'perhaps susceptible of something like proof'.[2] Why this uncharacteristic dithering twice over, with 'perhaps' and 'something like', as if there were something inherently obscure in the proof status of the doctrine? Doubtless to be assigned an a priori, rather than an a posteriori, status, the doctrine remains open to denial (so goes the subtext) without fear of outright inconsistency as a point of strict logic. How one might go about rejecting the doctrine has already been suggested by my sidelong glances towards theology. We may suppose there to be a possible world, W_{36}, in which God creates not one but ten different Adams (perhaps on ten different planets), all indistinguishable from one another and from Adam; one must then ask which of these Adams, if any, is truly Adam. Well, there is one peculiar property that does 'distinguish' Adam from his doubles, namely, that of being identical with Adam, which is not of course to be confused with the property of being self-identical, which everything possesses. This is the famous *haecceitas*, or this-ness, of Adam, which we associate above all with Duns Scotus in the fourteenth century, and which, in our day is defended forcefully by Alvin Plantinga in his *The Nature of Necessity*. The haecceity (or Socrateity) of Socrates may be supposed to be a function that picks Socrates out (as value) in each possible world (taken as argument) from which he is not absent; it is thus arguable that metaphysics as such culminates precisely in the Scotistic doctrine of haecceity, which alone succeeds in capturing the unshareable essence of each individual thing. However essential animality or rationality may be to Socrates, no such accumulation of Aristotelian essential properties could be expected to capture the very being of Socrates himself, Socrates *qua* Socrates, though the haecceities of the metaphysician do lend themselves to that end. Comparing and contrasting W_1 and W_{36}, only God's intuition is powerful enough to pierce through to the haecceity of Adam as it is instantiated twice over in the two worlds.

Going the Scotistic route, one is now free to insist that in W_4 our carpenter does succeed *Deo volente* in bringing about the instantiation of A's haecceity in the medium of D! For if Kripke's

[2] Saul Kripke, *Naming and Necessity* (Cambridge, Mass.: Harvard University Press, 1980), p. 114.

doctrine regarding the necessity of material origins reminds one of the medieval slogan 'Matter is the principle of individuation', one knows that Scotus's haecceities were expressly designed to supply a rival principle of trans-world individuation. How else explain God's decision to create Adam and not someone exactly like him? There is an inevitable irony in anyone's choosing to leap out of the Kripkean frying-pan into the Scotistic fire, as if almost no price were too high to pay to avoid conceding that the following are two essential properties of A: namely, having been made out of C and *not* having been made out of D. The embarrassment of our anti-essentialists can be brought out as follows. Of the two versions of anti-essentialism available, only one—the relativistic sort—is properly to be styled 'anti-metaphysical', but this one can readily be shown to be untenable, while the other version—namely, accidentalism—proves to be at least as 'metaphysical', in the pejorative sense of the term, as Aristotelian essentialism itself. The latter point first, for there are few anti-essentialist philosophers today who on being challenged fail to lapse quickly into accidentalism, which, give or take a theological nuance or two, is scarcely to be distinguished from Scotism.

Rather than admit that not being a pumpkin is an essential property of Socrates, they will press their one strong suit: namely, that the proposition expressed by 'The man Socrates was a pumpkin or at any rate something indistinguishable from a pumpkin during one phase of his career' cannot be shown to harbour a logical inconsistency. And they then feel committed to insisting that such an event really *could* have occurred. Well, suppose that during some early stage of its gestation the Socratic foetus, as a result of being bombarded with radiation, turned into a pumpkin-like thing, where I am assuming that the expression 'x turns into y' is semantically neutral as between cases where x is or is not identical with y. Would that thing be Socrates? On strong ground here, the Scotist is free to posit two physically indistinguishable worlds featuring that episode, in one of which the thing is Socrates, in the other not, with only God being capable of telling the two apart.

Anti-essentialism in its relativized form is summed up in Quine's statement 'Just insofar as we are talking referentially of the object, with no special bias toward a background grouping of mathematicians as against cyclists or vice versa, there is no semblance of sense in rating some of his attributes as necessary *and others as contingent*.'[3] Well, take Socrates under any description you please—say, as that bearded man pestering people in the Agora. Is being bearded, then, an essential property of that bearded man? Even allowing for some ambiguity as between a *de re* and a *de dicto* reading of the question, the answer must surely be no, if only because he was beardless as a boy; in any case, one can always test the hypothesis by shaving the bearded man to determine whether he can survive the outrage. So there are occasions when one verifies by an empirical test that a certain property belongs to a thing only accidentally, *absolutely speaking*, and not merely *qua F* or *qua G*. That there is, one must admit, a decisive asymmetry between the essential and the accidental features of a thing in respect to empirical testing merely serves to explain why our anti-essentialists are driven to become accidentalists.

If the putative metamorphosis of Socrates into a pumpkin proves that Frege's principle 'No entity without identity' must be seen to have a synthetic a priori status, at least when it comes to its modal application, that status also attaches to it in its non-modal uses. For in both cases the criterion of re-identification is required to be available to us, not merely to God. As to its non-modal uses, one has only to recall my 'theological conceit', inevitably welcome to the Scotist, whereby three sentences were found to express among them, bizarrely, two propositions.

It would be wrong of me to leave the impression that Kripke's doctrine regarding the necessity of origins is free of difficulties. Especially noteworthy is his insistence that Socrates could not possibly have had different parents. More precisely, the thesis is that he could not have come from a different sperm and a different egg, where we are inevitably assuming 'a rejection of the Cartesian picture'; for 'if we had a clear idea of the soul or the mind as an independent, subsistent, spiritual entity, why should it have to have any necessary connection with . . . a particular

---

[3] W. V. Quine, *Word and Object* (Cambridge, Mass.: MIT Press, 1960), p. 199 (my emphasis).

sperm or a particular egg'?[4] Let it be granted, then, that Socrates is a material object; even so, more is required if Kripke's position is to be fully convincing. Socrates must be a material object essentially, which is to say, in all possible worlds. That every material object is essentially such—that is, (x) x is a material object $\supset \square$ x is a material object—has probably never been doubted even by anti-essentialists! But once the issue is raised, and it is Plantinga to whom I am indebted here, the synthetic a priori pretensions of the proposition can only lead one to view it with the keenest suspicion before one can be expected to make one's peace with it.

How the distinction between body and soul has vexed the issue of personal identity from the beginning is already indicated in the opening lines of the *Iliad*, where the anger of Achilles is found to have dispatched to Hades the souls of many heroes, *themselves* being rendered thereby a prey for dogs and birds. So the hero himself is to be identified with his body, not his soul? Later in Plato's *Phaedo* the puzzle re-emerges as follows. When Socrates dies, his soul persists beyond the grave, but if Socrates is identical with his soul, his soul dies at the moment he dies, and any prospect of the soul's being *immortal* (no need to be an accomplished Latinist here) goes out the window. So Socrates is not identical with his soul (being perhaps a composite of body and soul)? But then the persistence of his soul fails to provide for the persistence of Socrates.

Waiving the issue of the soul, can it at least be said that a cat ceases to exist when it dies? Aristotle thought so, being committed to the proposition that (x) x is a cat $\supset \square$ x is alive. But we do readily enough *say* (for whatever it's worth) things like 'The cat was buried a day after it died,' suggesting that the speaker takes being alive to be merely an accidental feature of the cat. In a more serious vein it may perhaps be argued that a cat does continue to exist after it dies, but only for a very short time, until decomposition sets in. What does the science of biology have to say on the issue? Or would a conference of senior biologists convened to address the point prefer to table the motion that

[4] Kripke, op. cit., p. 155.

animals cease to exist when they die as being too 'metaphysical'? And hence as lying outside the bounds of science proper? So an experimental scientist who undertakes to keep a cat under steady observation throughout its career will not know whether he is entitled to leave off, when the cat dies? If the anti-essentialist is prone to revel in these puzzles, the maxim 'No entity without (diachronic) identity', at any rate when it is understood along Fregean (and Quinean) lines, might well be taken to lead to the consequence that there simply are no animals!

Death aside, birth is not without interest. His birth and death being stereotypically taken as defining the beginning and the end of a man's life (existence?), it is not to be doubted that a day before he is born a man is very much in existence, nor that he is alive on that day. It is thus surprising to find that when we speak metaphorically of the birth and death of the sun, say, we do seem to be operating on the tacit belief that being 'born', taken literally, involves coming into existence, though the death of the sun may allow for its continuance, depleted of all activity, as a black hulk. Only the grossest, most stereotypical sort of thinking could suppose that 'birth' and 'death', whether taken literally or metaphorically, signify polar opposites, and it is thus to be feared that we characteristically live our lives in a conceptual muddle. *Caveat poeta!* Those being among the most potent metaphors that we live (and die) by, the clarification of our very lives may be expected to require the poet as well as the metaphysician, the one taking over where the other leaves off.

Part V

22

Causation

Referring expressly to Hume's critique of a 'single but important concept in metaphysics, namely that of the connection of cause and effect', Kant is famous for writing: 'Since the origin of metaphysics so far as we know its history, nothing has ever happened which could have been more decisive to its fate.' Closer to home, if it was the emergence in our time of ZF intuition that occasioned my reopening the whole issue of the synthetic a priori, the Kripkean renewal of essentialism is even more manifestly importunate in calling us to reopen this issue of causation, particularly with regard to an earlier discussion of Kant, in which he says of Hume, 'He could not explain how it can be possible that the understanding must think concepts, which are not in themselves connected in the understanding'—there is no *de dicto* necessity here—'as being necessarily connected in the object'—that is to say, *de re*. Essence and causation can thus be viewed jointly as involving, quite apart from any link in our concepts, a necessary connection between one item out in the world and another, where the two items in the one case are a thing and one of its properties, and in the other an event and its cause. Because physicality as such might well be supposed to be constituted in some decisive fashion by one mode of causation or another, metaphysics in the specific form of meta-physics (looking no further) can hardly refrain from addressing the topic.

After more than two centuries of developments, the Humean problematic is probably canvassed nowhere more adequately than in J. L. Mackie's study of the topic, always allowing for his own Humean convictions. On one point at least, Mackie is persuaded that 'Hume's argument is conclusive and beyond question'—namely, in his insistence that when it comes to cause and effect 'there are no logically necessary connections between the events themselves, or between any *intrinsic* description of them, however detailed'.[1] With malice aforethought, we may take as an example the boiling of a pot of water thanks to its being very hot, precisely because it invites us to exploit Kripke's essentialist account of heat. If the cause here may be picked out by such expressions as 'the great heat of the water' or 'the water's being very hot', the effect is felicitously identified by 'the water's being (highly) agitated' rather than 'the water's boiling', for the latter description might well be taken to imply that the water is hot when no such merely verbal victory could satisfy us.

Picked out, then, by 'concepts which are not in themselves connected in the understanding'—namely, the concepts 'heat' and 'agitation'—it is 'the events themselves' that inevitably concern us and whose 'intrinsic descriptions' as supplied in Kripkean terms will be found to indicate not only (a) how the two concepts can be 'necessarily connected in the object' (the water) and (b) how there can be a logically necessary connection between those descriptions, but also (c) how there can be a logically necessary connection between the events themselves. Casting about for an intrinsic description of the cause, we are led to ask what the water's being very hot might consist in, intrinsically; and the answer here can only be this: the rapid motion of the molecules which compose the water. In the same vein, looking for an intrinsic description of the effect, we are eager to learn what the water's being (highly) agitated might consist in; here again the answer lies ready to hand: the rapid motion of the molecules which compose the water. No wonder, then, that there is a logically necessary connection between cause and effect, seeing that they are identical; and whatever Scotistic reservations one might have about Kripke's doctrine regarding the necessity of origins, much more fundamental is his doctrine concerning the necessity of identity (and diversity)—namely, that (a) $(x)(y) x = y \supset \Box x = y$ and that (b) $(x)(y) \sim (x = y) \supset \Box \sim (x = y)$. It is this latter principle that warrants our conviction that if (as we suppose) Benjamin Franklin and George Washington are distinct in the actual world (unlike the Morning Star and the Evening Star), they are distinct in every possible world, with the consequence that an

[1] J. L. Mackie, *The Cement of the Universe: A Study in Causation* (Oxford: Clarendon Press, 1974), p. 17; emphasis original.

essential feature of Franklin is to be found in his not being (identical with) Washington.

Vital to our essentialist account of causation, Kripke's use of 'the necessity of identity' to insist that heat = (rapid) molecular motion must be eked out by specifically linguistic considerations; there is thus some (small) justification for fearing that a metaphysical rabbit is being pulled out of a linguistic hat by both of us. We call something 'hot' if it causes in us certain sensations (heat sensations) when we touch it; it has thus been too readily supposed that 'the water is hot' could only mean 'the water causes in us heat sensations when we touch it'. It is not the meaning of the sentence that is decisive, however, but rather its semantics—that is to say, its truth conditions. Following Kripke, I take as invalid the argument: 'The water is hot. Therefore, the water causes heat sensations in us when we touch it.' For there is a possible world where the premiss is true and the conclusion false. In that world the water may cause in us cold sensations even while remaining hot, so long as it has that property (rapid motion of its molecules) which in this world causes in us heat sensations. In sharp contrast the following argument *is* valid: 'The water is hot. Therefore, its molecules are in rapid motion.' Even so, knowing that the premiss of the argument is true fails to suffice when it comes to knowing that the conclusion is true. Taking the two arguments together, the one invalid, the other valid, we come to realize that if the conclusion of the former indicates an accidental feature of heat, the conclusion of the latter specifies an essential one. Although the accidental feature is not definitive of the meaning of the word 'heat', it does play a decisive role in 'fixing its reference', in Kripke's apt phrase, where it emerges that what the word 'heat' in fact picks out in an object is its rapid molecular motion, to which we must accordingly turn for our 'intrinsic description' of the phenomenon. In much the same way, 'the number of planets' picks out an object—namely, 9—by one of its accidental features.

'To know its essential nature', writes Aristotle in *Posterior Analytics*, 2. 8. 93a4–5, 'is the same as to know the cause of a thing's existence', and his accompanying discussion suggests that he is guided principally by the fact that in reply to each of the questions What is the cause of lightning? and What *is* (the essential nature of) lightning?, we hesitate not at all in saying, 'An electrical discharge'. Very puzzling in the context of post-Humean discussions, Aristotle's linking of essence and causation can be readily seen to anticipate my own approach; though the easiest way of reconciling Hume and Aristotle might be to argue that, while the one addresses only cases in which the cause precedes the effect in time, the other confines himself to those in which they are not only simultaneous but even identical. 'The great majority of efficient natural causes', one may be surprised to find Kant writing in his most thematic encounter with Hume, 'are simultaneous with their effects,' which at least serves to discourage one in advance from undertaking to package Hume and Aristotle together in some rough-and-ready fashion.

If the Aristotelian response to Hume may be termed essentialist in emphasis, the Kantian one can only be styled 'transcendental' in import, though *what* Kant's argument against Hume might be supposed to consist in remains perplexingly obscure. Even the most seductive version of it available today, Arthur Melnick's in his *Kant's Analogies of Experience*, could hardly be expected to give more than momentary pause to a Humean like Mackie. A neo-Humean actually, Mackie remains faithful to the spirit of his master's text, even while (probably) violating its letter when he insists that 'singular causal statements cannot be true . . . as we ordinarily mean them'.[2] The difficulty here turns on the counterfactual feature of causation; on Mackie's account, statements of the form '*x* caused *y*' are to be analyzed (waiving complications) as being equivalent to statements of the form '*x* occurred and *y* occurred and in the circumstances *y* would not have occurred if *x* had not'. What it is, then, for a stone striking a window to *cause* it to shatter consists above all in the failure of the window to shatter in every possible world exactly like the actual one except for the stone striking it. For 'statements of singular causal sequence involve in their analysis counterfactual conditionals which . . . state what would have happened not what did happen' by appealing to 'possible situations or possible worlds', and 'which on the present showing are

---

[2] Mackie, *The Cement of the Universe*, pp. 54, 229.

not capable of being true', though they may be 'acceptable or unacceptable, well or poorly supported and so on'. Even more to the point, 'causal statements, though not themselves true, are surrogates for clusters of statements which can be true', where those clusters feature Humean regularities that invite one to extrapolate from known to unknown cases by means of induction. Although some counterfactuals do succeed in being literally true—for example, 'If the number of planets had been ten rather than nine, the number of planets would have been even and not odd'—where a necessary connection obtains between the relevant concepts, it is precisely the absence of any such perspicuous link when it comes to causation that renders Mackie quite incapable of understanding how *these* counterfactuals—the opaque, as opposed to the transparent variety—could possibly be true. Quite as mandatory in the case of essential properties, as in the case of causation, the opaque counterfactual serves as a *tertium quid* which negotiates between the two themes; as such, it can be seen to carry us further towards first principles than either of the themes taken separately.

Generous enough to concede that there may be a synthetic a priori kind of necessity involved in colour incompatibilities of the red/green sort, Mackie observes that 'nothing in this example helps us to see what could be conjectured about a necessity linking two distinct occurrences'.[3] Well, what about Kripke's necessities of origin? If, on the one hand, this table is not identical with the wood of which it is composed, and if, on the other, it could not possibly have been made from any other (quantity of) wood, have we not here an intelligible necessity linking two (logically) distinct items? Logically distinct not in the sense that either can exist in the absence of the other but in the sense that 6 is distinct from 7. Granted that such a necessity is intelligible in the case in which x is the material cause of y (for that is what Kripke's doctrine comes to in Aristotelian jargon), what about the case in which x is the efficient cause of y? Even Mackie might allow that Kripke 'helps us to see what could be *conjectured* about a necessity linking two distinct occurrences' that are related as cause to effect, and at least some of the sting is removed from Hume's

[3] Ibid., pp. 54, 55, 37, 49, 216, 230.

insistence that 'we have no idea of this connection nor even any distinct notion of what we desire to know when we endeavour at a conception of it'. Precisely what we are endeavouring at a conception *of* can be described only as tantalizing in the etymological sense of the word, and after Kripke we can be said almost to taste it.

As to how we might actually grasp it, a clue is supplied by an uncharacteristic lapse in scholarship in Mackie when he writes, 'It would be strange if . . . a causal theory of perception . . . turned out to be an a priori truth,'[4] evincing no awareness of H. P. Grice's influential paper on the topic, which has convinced many philosophers, myself included, of that 'strange' thing.[5] Suppose now that we are right in believing that perception entails causation. Suppose Mackie is also right in his conviction that 'singular causal statements cannot be true . . . as we ordinarily mean them'. So there is then no causation, properly speaking, and *a fortiori* no perception either, with the further consequence that our fancied knowledge of the external world is also nullified; here I have only to allude to the causal theory of knowledge, which dominates epistemology today, in order to reinforce the point. 'But this is outright scepticism,' someone can be heard to murmur, 'which can hardly provide material to be used against Hume.' True enough, but such a response would be much too short-sighted. Excelling in piecemeal analysis, analytical philosophy rewards us with Mackie on causation, Grice on perception, Alvin Goldman on knowledge,[6] and so on, but when it comes to any synoptic vision encompassing these independent studies there is a striking poverty. How else explain the failure to reopen the whole issue of scepticism along the lines suggested?

It should be evident that scepticism is only one of the options available, and my primary intent in fact is to run the argument in reverse, though it turns out to be memory, not perception, that is the more promisingly adapted to that end. Here it is

---

4 Mackie, *The Cement of the Universe*, p. 111.

5 H. P. Grice, 'The Causal Theory of Perception', *Proceedings of the Aristotelian Society*, supp. vol. 35 (1961).

6 A. Goldman, 'A Causal Theory of Knowledge', *Journal of Philosophy*, 64 (1967): 357–725.

'Remembering' by C. B. Martin and M. Deutscher (*Philosophical Review*, 75 (1966)) on which I rely for a key premiss in (one version of) my argument—namely, that memory also entails causation. The goal is to convince Mackie, and above all Hume, how it is that a counterfactual of the opaque variety could possibly be true, though it should be emphasized that the mnemonic version of my general line of argument is only one of several that can be recommended. All versions, however, call upon the deep modal principle 'Actuality entails possibility', for each undertakes to show that at least one opaque counterfactual is actually true. I assume that anyone brought to concede as much is obliged to withdraw his psuedo-query (it is in fact a form of protest) 'But how *could* such a counterfactual ever be true?' Basically, the argument turns out to be none other than Kant's 'transcendental deduction' of causality at the heart of which lies the famous 'synthetic unity of apperception'.

Take the simple judgement 'This pain is increasing in intensity'. The object (of reference) is the pain of which increase in intensity is being currently predicated by me. If the judgement is to express knowledge, Kant writes that we must be 'conscious that what we think'—namely, the object—'is the same as what we thought a moment before'—in its own way perhaps an instance of 'No entity without (diachronic) identity'—for an earlier and later state of the object must be compared and contrasted, which requires more than mere perception—that is, sensory awareness —at each instant, but apperception over an interval of time as well. More precisely, memory of the earlier state is imperative if a 'synthetic unity' is to be achieved whereby the later state can be compared with it. But memory entails causation, and any episode of causation entails the truth of at least one opaque counterfactual. Accordingly, we come to understand, albeit in the most roundabout sort of way, how there can be a necessary connection between one episode, the cause, and another, the effect, even though it can never be made transparent to mind as such; for Hume's demand that 'we must produce some instance wherein the efficacy is plainly discoverable to the mind' cannot be satisfied.

An anti-realist as regards causal episodes, Mackie is found to be an anti-realist regarding possible worlds as well. For though 'statements of singular causal sequence involve in their analysis counterfactual conditionals', where 'these counterfactual conditionals describe possible situations or possible worlds', we are cautioned that 'such talk about possibilities (or possible worlds) must not be taken too literally: to talk about them is still only to talk about our supposings and how we develop them; possible worlds other than the actual one have no fully objective existence.'[7] Double-talk, on the Quinean ground that a philosopher is once again helping himself to certain abstract entities even while disowning them? No. In his *analysis* of causal statements, Mackie is entitled to invoke any hobgoblin of his choice—opaque necessities, possible worlds, and so on—as long as he is satisfied that such statements are never 'true in a strict sense'. Accepting his analysis of those statements, I can now put the mnemonic deduction of causality to a further use, by insisting on the strength of it that there are possible worlds and *a fortiori* abstract entities after all. This consequence is all the more to be welcomed in the face of Paul Benacerraf's recent challenge to Platonists to explain how, in the absence of any causal interaction with their transcendent objects, they have come to learn of their existence. We can now answer as follows. If the way we come to know of things is through causal interaction with them, notably in the form of sense perception, there is an evident need to understand what might be the ingredients of causation itself. Suppose now that the occurrence of causal episodes could be shown to presuppose the existence of abstract entities in the specific form of possible worlds, along the lines of Mackie's account, where 'counterfactual conditionals describe possible situations or possible worlds'. We can then argue, 'The stone broke the window, therefore there are abstract entities.' Ironically, in some unexpected fashion we thus come to know of their existence on the basis of certain causal episodes.

If the mnemonic deduction of causality comes closest to Kant's transcendental programme with its stress on the synthetic unity of apperception, there are other versions of the argument, taken

---

[7] Mackie, *The Cement of the Universe*, p. 199.

more generally, which have their own appeal. Trading on the private langauge argument, widely acknowledged to be the most important piece of sustained transcendental reasoning since Kant, the semiotic version harks back beyond Wittgenstein to Hume himself. If the mind never perceives any real connection between distinct existences, how do words *refer* to sensations? There are two distinct existences here, the sensation-token, the pain in my foot, and the word-token, 'pain', which I am presumably using to refer to the sensation-token. But how is the connection between the name and the thing set up? Even more to the point, how can there so much as *be* a (real) connection between the two items for me to recognize as such? Has not Hume shown that no such connection is so much as thinkable? In Kantian terms, how is it possible to think an object, or equivalently, yet more concretely (in Wittgenstein's idiom), to apply a word to it? Merely to invoke the non-natural relation of meaning—'x means or refers to y'—serves only to label the puzzle. Suppose, then, that I inscribe the word 'pain' in my diary every time I am in pain. The Humean regularity with which the one item accompanies the other cannot be purely accidental if it is indeed the case that the relation of meaning or reference obtains between them. Each sensation-token must cause—must at any rate serve as a causal factor in bringing about—the attendant word-token, which is not by any means to say that the causal process is somehow phenomenologically available to consciousness. Nor will it suffice to suggest that the pain merely serves as the reason, not the cause, of the word-token. If the argument 'I refer to my pain with the word "pain"', therefore there is at least one law of nature' proves now to be valid by virtue of Hume's maxim 'No causality without universality', the validity belongs rather to transcendental than to formal logic. *What* the law of nature might be I do not know. It is a mere caricature to suppose it to be a rule to the effect that whenever I am in pain I write 'pain', though the caricature is not without its usefulness as a first approximation, as much as to say in the Humean case that windows shatter when hit by stones.

Deeper than either the semiotic or the mnemonic deductions of causality, each of which is content to exploit some limited aspect of mind, the dispositional deduction covers a whole range of

cases, which variously proceed from such premises as 'Achilles
is irascible,' 'Achilles is angry,' 'I am angry,' and 'I fear (hope,
believe) that it will rain in the next hour' to the omnibus conclusion that something is disposed to behave in certain ways in
certain counterfactual circumstances, beyond which lie in the
background universal laws of nature and necessary, albeit
opaque, connections between different sorts of episodes. Associated above all with the name of Ryle, the dispositional account
of mind was touched on in Chapters 7, 12, and 19; and if behavi-
ourists have used it as their mainstay, no one any longer appears
to doubt its cogency when it comes to such relatively modest
truths as that belief, desire, fear, and so on have a dispositional
component to them, whatever else they may consist in. Strikingly,
however, the synthetic a priori status of any such truth—one can
deny it without fear of inconsistency—has gone unnoticed, if
only because one has innocently supposed that the tough-minded
behaviourist could never be convicted of anything so tender-
minded as the synthetic a priori.

How tough-minded to the point of incoherence Ryle's final
position proves to be, one comes to appreciate only after dis-
covering that he is combining a dispositional account of mind
with an anti-realist account of dispositions! A small point first.
'It is a publicly ascertainable *fact* about a field', writes Ryle, 'that
it is green, i.e. that it *would* look so and so to anyone in a position
to see it properly'.[8] Innocuous in itself, this incidental remark
needs to be juxtaposed with a fairly extended passage in which
Ryle undertakes to rebut the charge that his 'whole programme of
talking about capacities, tendencies, liabilities and pronenesses'
in his critique of 'the ghost in the machine' merely involves
trading one sort of occult entity for another.

Potentialities, it is truistically said, are nothing actual. . . . To say of a
sleeping man that he can read French, or of a piece of dry sugar that it is
soluble in water, seems to be pretending at once to accord an attribute
and to put that attribute in cold storage. . . . This is a valid objection to
one kind of account of such statements . . ., namely an account which
construes such statements as asserting extra matters of fact. This was

---

8 G. Ryle, *The Concept of Mind* (London: Hutchinson, 1949), p. 220; emphasis added.

indeed the mistake of the old Faculty theories which construed dispositional words as denoting occult agencies or causes, i.e. things existing, or processes taking place, in a sort of limbo world. But the truth that sentences containing words like 'might', 'could' and 'would . . . if' do not report limbo facts does not entail that such sentences have not got proper jobs of their own to perform. The job of reporting matters of fact is only one of a wide range of sentence-jobs.[9]

A tendentious, even precious, use of the word 'fact'? No. Ryle means what he says. A purely factual account of grass is prohibited from describing it as green or even as being such that it would look so to anyone *if* he were in a position to see it properly. But this purge of all the so-called secondary qualities is only the thin end of the wedge. Mind itself drops out of any purely factual account of the world, leaving only bodies in motion, as Ryle emerges as an eliminative materialist. Well, that may not be quite fair. Some mental items, like sensations of pain, may count as hard matters of fact, but that reduces Ryle to being an old-fashioned Cartesian dualist.

Quine writes:

There are those who uncritically accept the dispositional idiom as a clear matter of ordinary language. Say what a thing is disposed to do in what circumstances, and the disposition holds no further mystery for them. . . . Such is Ryle's position in *The Concept of Mind*, where he undertakes to clarify other more obscure and troublesome notions in dispositional terms and is content to leave them thus.[10]

As a piece of textual exegesis, Quine's reading of Ryle is wide of the mark, but on a deeper level he is right. That his anti-realist account of dispositions might commit him to an anti-realist account of mind, Ryle appears never to have suspected. It is Quine, with his eyes wide open, who has taken that plunge into eliminative materialism; and I submit that if one is bent on rejecting my ultra-realist, transcendental deduction of causality, in any of its three versions, one has no other choice but to go the Quinean route, where after guilefully construing mind in dispositional terms, one then has no qualms in banishing all dispositions from one's austere ontology.

9 Ibid., pp. 119-20.
10 W. V. Quine, *The Roots of Reference* (La Salle, Ill.: Open Court, 1974), p. 9.

23

Anti-realism

If one is an anti-realist about F's—let them be dispositions, causal episodes, possible worlds, colours, minds, bodies, or anything else that might interest philosophers—one is prepared to deny that there really (the operative word) are any such things. But that is only one of two criteria that must be satisfied. Otherwise we should all be anti-realists about mermaids. Mere disbelief in mermaids is not enough. One must also allow oneself to be at least nominally committed to the existence of F's, as we all are to numbers. For the anti-realist is precisely that: a nominalist, for he insists that his commitment to F's (numbers or whatever) is merely nominal. No mere historical accident, it is the medieval debate over universals, pitting 'nominalists' against 'realists', that has come in our time to be generalized so as to apply to any value of F whatever. Willing enough to *say* 'Socrates has wisdom', the medieval nominalist was prone to insist that if he was nominally committed to the existence of wisdom as well as to that of Socrates, it was only to Socrates that his ontological commitment should be seen to extend. Here, then, we have a model of what being an anti-realist regarding any particular value of F might consist in, and there is, in fact, no value of F regarding which some philosopher of recent times has not taken an anti-realist line.

Although it is typically the case that one is an anti-realist about F's only because one is very much a realist about G's, it may yet be asked what it might be like for someone to be an anti-realist about everything—that is to say, a nihilist. That there are no mermaids, absolutely speaking, I take to be granted by all parties from the outset, *pace* Meinong; and seeing that it would be altogether unsuitable for any of us to be characterized as anti-realists regarding mermaids, terminological considerations alone recommend that with respect to mermaids, phlogiston, the ether, and so on even the most radical anti-realist among us is to be classified as a realist. 'You are assuming then', someone can be heard to protest, 'that we can be absolutely certain that there are no mermaids anywhere in the universe.' Not at all. Suitable enough in epistemology, doubts about mermaids are simply out of place when it comes to the purely metaphysical issue of realism versus anti-realism, and here I am thinking of local as well as global anti-realism. The global anti-realist or nihilist, as we may now redefine him, is one who, even while being fully satisfied, metaphysically speaking, that some statements of the form 'There are no F's' are just plain true without any qualification, refuses to accord that privilege to any statement of the form 'There are F's'. Although some statements of that form will be allowed to be true relative to this or that viable (or valid) conceptual scheme, they are all found to be false relative to some other such scheme. By no means permissive, the standard for viability or validity when it comes to conceptual schemes is summed up in the phrase 'scientifically adequate'. How two logically incompatible theories of the world can both qualify as scientifically adequate as well as pragmatically equivalent, one recalls from Chapter 16, where statements featuring points (regions) were glossed in terms of sets of regions (points). Much to be deplored, however, is the readiness with which even self-styled realist philosophers today tend to concede that there may well be no 'fact of the matter' as to which of the two theories (punctual versus regional) is true to the exclusion of the other, as if one's dialectical resources were simply exhausted. One would surely wish to know whether a moving particle in physics might be allowed with the exiguous 'magnitude' of a mere mathematical point before knuckling under to the anti-realist, for if such a particle is properly conceivable, spatial points must be available to accommodate it.

In practice there appears to be only one reliable bulwark against nihilism, and that is one's confidence in either Aristotelian or Cartesian entities, the one consisting of medium-sized public particulars like cats and dogs or even mountains and rivers, the other comprising subjective items like sensations. Both sorts of entity have been subjected to sharp attacks in recent years

by realists of one persuasion or another, leaving only the nihilist
to profit from the carnage. For one has only to become a local
anti-realist regarding Cartesian as well as Aristotelian entities,
and there are few today who can resist the further pull to nihilism,
otherwise and more benignly termed 'pragmatism'. Although
there is no reason in principle why a realist might not be content
to be a local anti-realist or nominalist regarding every (suitable)
value of *F* that has come to his attention, insisting only that he
cannot be expected to believe that nothing whatever exists, absolutely speaking, any such position would be regarded by contemporary philosophers as very strange. In the years ahead, however,
as discussions like the present one become more familiar, the
position may even be felt to be almost routinely plausible.

How anti-realism regarding Cartesian entities can come to
seem compelling may be brought out in easy stages, with particular reference to an especially obstinate item, pain. Kripke's example here is instructive. Satisfied that we are (essentially) material objects, Kripke remains enough of a mentalist, despite his
'rejection of the Cartesian picture', to insist that being a pain
cannot be supposed to be a merely accidental feature of any pain,
and in the same vein he fails to understand how his own strategy,
effective enough when it comes to the proposition 'Heat =
molecular motion', could be used to vindicate the conviction
of Australian materialists, notably J. J. C. Smart and D. M.
Armstrong, that some such an identity as 'Pain = stimulation of
C-fibres' can be supposed to be true. That pain just is (essentially)
pain, irreducible to anything physical, can thus be felt to coerce
one into being a realist at least about that one thing. Showing that
no pain is essentially a pain might be expected to be rather more
difficult than merely showing, as I did in Chapter 6, that no wind
is essentially a wind. Suppose, however, that tormented by a
raging toothache, you come to be distracted from it by a sudden
emergency that calls on all your powers. Triumphing, you turn at
leisure to enjoy the plaudits of the crowd, when once again the
toothache crashes back into your consciousness. Did the toothache cease to exist during the interim when you were absorbed in
your rescue operation? Granted that you ceased to be aware of it
at the time, is this a case in which Berkeley's *esse est percipi* must

be conceded to hold? Let us at any rate concede this much, that throughout the interim the toothache ceased to be an ache, a pain, on the strength of (1).

(1) $(x) (y) (x$ is a pain $\cdot\ y$ has $x) \supset y$ is aware of x.

Must the pain then *a fortiori* have ceased to exist? Call the toothache 'Jones'. At time t_1 Jones is very much a pain sensation; at t_2 we suppose Jones to persist, but not as a pain sensation; but at t_3 Jones is once more a pain. We are thus undertaking to deny (3) even while acquiescing in (2).

(2) $\Box\ (x)\ x$ is a pain $\supset x$ is a pain.
(3) $(x)\ x$ is a pain $\supset \Box\ x$ is a pain.

Alternatively, if perhaps somewhat less plausibly, Jones may remain a pain during t_2 but, in defiance of (1), a pain of which you ceased to be conscious. On either version, being an item of consciousness no longer counts as an essential property of a pain; though on the more plausible version it is acknowledged—here I am speaking *de dicto* rather than *de re*—that it is essential to any pain *qua* being a pain that it be an item of consciousness. By no means coercive, the story I take to have a certain inherent attractiveness, not least of all when it is asked whether it accords phenomenologically with the introspective data of consciousness itself. Viewed purely introspectively, one may well feel Jones to be an objective item that can be supposed to persist even during the interval when all of one's attention is directed elsewhere. So much of the contemporary case for a materialist account of mind can seem to rest on an outright contempt for any such introspective data that the present discussion may be felt to be fairly novel. For it will be evident that if a pain can exist without being an item of consciousness, it can hardly fail to be something physical, in the absence of any plausible third possibility.

Precisely what physical item the pain might be can be brought out as follows. When a man cries out in pain, it is presumably the pain that causes him to cry out. Suppose now that a physiologist determines that the cause of his crying out is the stimulation of his C-fibres. What to do? How shall we reconcile these rival accounts? But why suppose that there is any rivalry here? The facts seem to be summed up by (4).

(4) The man's pain = the cause of his crying out = the stimulation of his C-fibres.

On the face of it, what we have here are three co-referential, definite descriptions, and one need only appeal to the transitivity of identity in order to deduce that the man's pain is just (identical with) the stimulation of his C-fibres. As Fregeans, we cannot but welcome this opportunity to recognize one and the same object under two different modes of presentation, once as a pain and once as the stimulation of C-fibres. There is, moreover, a third mode of presentation, whereby the object is 'given' us, as Frege says, namely, as the sense of the singular term 'the cause of his crying out'.

Readily assimilated to the Fregean framework of ontology, as we have come to characterize it, 'Australian' materialism accommodates itself even more closely to the format of Kripkean essentialism. No more instructive paradigm of the new essentialism can be found than (5), which will be seen to be almost exactly on a par with (4).

(5) The heat of this body = whatever it is in this body that causes heat sensations in us when we touch it = the motion of molecules in this body.

There is indeed this difference between (5) and (4), though both have the form 'the F = the G = the H': in the case of (5) we know that the F is identical with the G purely on the strength of a nominal definition. What we mean by the word 'heat' is stipulated to be whatever it is that causes this sort of sensation in us. No such triviality allows us to identify the F and the G in the case of (4), where empirical fact comes into play. If it is on a somewhat more advanced level, then, that (4) exemplifies the Kripkean strategy operative in (5), they are both very much on a par in instantiating Frege's vision into (6) and (7).

(6) $5 + 7 = 12$.
(7) The Morning Star = The Evening Star.

Only recently, in the last two decades perhaps, has it become clear precisely what Frege was after in juxtaposing (6) and (7). Originally persuaded that in order to refute Kant it was enough to prove that the truths of arithmetic were analytic, Frege came to realize, presciently as it turns out, that the widespread view regarding 'the sterility of logic' would have to be addressed independently, on its own ground. In (6) quite as much as (7), though the former is known to be true on an a priori, the latter on an a posteriori basis, one and the same object is recognized twice over under different modes of presentation, and thus epistemic synthesis—Kant was right to insist on this—can be seen to take place even in the case of a logically analytic proposition where, indeed, '5 + 7 = 9 + 3' serves perhaps as a more felicitous example of the point in question.

That there is such an *object* as the pain in my foot, to which we refer, of which we predicate, and over which we quantify, the materialist is almost as prepared to accept as any mentalist. But it is precisely at this point that the anti-realist comes specifically into his own, in connection with (8) and (9):

(8) I have an excruciating pain in my foot.
(9) My foot hurts excruciatingly.

Interchangeable for all practical purposes, (8) and (9) differ in their explicit ontological commitments, in that the former involves reference to three objects (me, my pain, and my foot), one of which (the pain) drops out of the latter, though one is always free to insist that (9) is merely an elliptical version of (8). Disdaining all such merely linguistic considerations, one may happily concede that (9) differs from (8) in its ontological import, just as it agrees with it in its pragmatic import, even while insisting that as a plain matter of fact (language aside) one is indubitably aware of the object in question; namely, the pain in one's foot. If our anti-realist must fight shy of all such so-called Cartesian intuitions, Descartes himself took pain to be a confused idea, and it may even be consonant with his thinking to argue that once (9) is allowed to be true, there is no great need to acquiesce in the reification of pain in (8). Conceding it for the nonce, however, there remains the following difficulty. Suppose that the pain is (as we say) increasing in intensity over the interval of time from t_1 to t_2. Nominally committed to such a perduring object, mentalists have in fact tended to suppose that a different sensation, and hence a different object, was being encountered at each instant, though here again the anti-realist will urge that even God could not be expected to resolve the issue.

Mentalism aside, *what* the number of objects might be in the world at large the nihilist takes to vary from one valid conceptual scheme to another, and already in Chapter 6 a kind of number anti-realism was found to be implicit in Thales. When it comes specifically to Aristotelian objects, two sorts of metaphysical doubt arise, summed up in the words 'supervenience' and 'sorites', which are particularly apposite. Recalling the first sort from Chapter 17, the issue is to be framed as a more or less technical one of logic. From a description of the world that mentions only rocks, trees, soil, streams, and so on, all of which I take to be emergent entities that arise on levels lower (in the ZF sense) than that on which mountains figure, along with the geometric and causal relations that obtain among them, can the existence of at least one mountain be deduced? Fiendishly complicated by collateral issues that might take a century to unravel, the question can be replaced by another that, while undertaking to press home the same point, can be *fairly* easily answered. Should we accept as valid the following argument? 'Dozens of cows were found grazing in *an elongate depression . . . (with an outlet) between . . . ranges of . . . mountains*, therefore there is at least one valley.' Well, yes, given that I lifted the quoted material from the nearest dictionary to hand where the word 'valley' is so defined. Even after all allowances are made, however, there remains an evident difficulty. Although philosophers standardly assume today that our common-sense ontology quantifies almost as readily over valleys as over mountains, elongate depressions are felt to be another matter entirely. Suppose, then, we accept the truth of the premiss subject to one restriction—namely, that while we are ontologically committed by it to cows and mountains, we are exempt from any such commitment to elongate depressions and *ranges* of mountains. To elongate depressions in particular we are then only nominally committed according to our Quinean poetics, which glosses the premiss as being in that regard infected with the rhetorical trope of reification, itself perhaps to be classified as a form of hyperbole. The premiss being construed now partly in anti-realist terms, I am very doubtful that the argument can be certified as valid, assuming of course that the conclusion is to be given a realist reading. As anti-realists about elongate depressions, we may even be motivated by an uneasy fear of inconsistency to extend our anti-realism to valleys as well. Admittedly, these notions of validity and inconsistency, manageable enough within the confines of formal logic, cannot be said to be affording us the clearest guidance here where, generalizing from the immediate point at issue, all emergent entities are now being put in question.

Much less exotic, sorites-type objections to Aristotelian objects take two forms, one superficial and merely 'ideological' in Quine's jargon, the other deep and properly ontological. One, two, three, and so on molecules being deleted from Mt. Everest, when exactly does it cease to be a mountain? But that is a mere matter of ideology, having to do with when the idea 'mountain' might cease to apply to the case at hand. Continuing to delete molecules, at some point we will be left with a mere hill before us, and that might yet be Everest, for we have no right simply to assume that being a mountain is an essential property of any mountain. The ontological question then is not when Everest ceases to be an F or a G, but when it ceases to be at all; and that question being limited here to sorites-type considerations turns out to be merely a special case of the more general issue regarding what features of Everest are to be taken as essential to it. At this point anti-essentialist misgivings prove to be more properly described as anti-realist reservations about Everest itself. Generalizing, it can even be argued that being an anti-essentialist about F's always entails, ultimately, being an anti-realist about them. An anti-essentialist when it comes to tables, Locke was, I submit, an essentialist regarding their sensible qualities. Take the quality this table has of being dark brown, and consider the full range of *its* properties, some of which—for example, being dark rather than light—Locke never doubts to be essential to it. As an ultra-realist regarding the sensible qualities of things, the Lockean comes to despair of the thing that has those qualities, and his anti-essentialism regarding the thing proves in the end to be scarcely distinguishable from his anti-realism towards it. Appealing in effect to 'No entity without identity', Butchvarov in his *Being qua Being* revives the Lockean position—except that each quality figures now as a universal, recurring at different times and places—precisely on the ground that when it comes to the full range of puzzles concerning diachronic identity (if the sorites paradox is one, the metamorphosis of a caterpillar into a butterfly indicates another), criteria adequate to resolve them are simply not to be found, even as regards the elementary particles of physics, let alone common-sense objects like mountains. Implicitly ruled out is the Scotistic (and accidentalist) suggestion that Socrates, who is conceded to be a man who died and even ceased to exist in 399 BC, might just happen to be this current itch in my foot. Socrates *redux*! Following Frege, the criteria of re-identification that must attend the use of a proper name like 'Socrates' are required to be available to those who assign and thereafter use the name.

If reification of qualities is one way of responding to anti-essentialist misgivings about diachronic identity, Quine in effect proposes another when he explains that the 'physical objects' in his austere ontology 'are not to be distinguished from events', for 'each comprises the content, however heterogeneous, of some portion of space-time, however disconnected and gerry-mandered'.[1] One such deviant physical object will be the mereo-logical sum of the first and the last pages in this book *at this instant* or during some (connected or disconnected) 5-minute interval of time. Although one might suppose that 'the content' of my right hand at this instant, t_1—namely, the stew of blood, bone, molecules, atoms, electrons, and so on found in my hand then—might turn out by a very long shot to be identical with the content of the same hand *now* at t_2, this thought, albeit natural enough, fails to respect Quine's insistence that physical objects 'are not to be distinguished from events'. There being no chance that the earlier event could be identical with the later one, puzzles concerning diachronic identity simply cannot arise in Quine's

[1] W. V. Quine, *Word and Object* (Cambridge, Mass.: MIT Press, 1960), p. 171.

universe. Not that his physical objects really are events, for he says that they are rather to be characterized as *process-things*, which are 'not to be identified either with the processes which things undergo *or* with the things which undergo them'. A misbegotten hybrid, this *tertium quid* towards which Quine is gesturing I can regard only with the keenest doubts as to its intelligibility, though his motivation I understand well enough. In any case, Mt. Everest cannot be identified with any object in Quine's ontology, if only because the vagueness of its boundaries, temporal as well as spatial, invites infinitely many process-things, each crisply articulated in space and time, to serve with equal right as its surrogate. Once again, then, Quine's two maxims, 'Explication is elimination' and 'No entity without identity', work as a team, the latter being invoked in the service of the former.

More recently, Quine invites us to 'imagine two neighboring electrons' and to 'consider the question whether some given point event and some later one belong together as moments in the career of the same electron or belong rather to different electrons', where 'quantum mechanics teaches, I think, that this question will sometimes lack physical meaning'. Appealing tacitly here to the principle 'No entity without diachronic identity', Quine suggests that 'the notion of a particle was only a rough conceptual aid' toward the understanding of 'nature', which is 'better conceived as a distribution of local states over space-time'. The world then consists entirely of a 'distribution of various quantitative states over regions of space-time', where 'the regions would be identified with . . . sets of quadruples of numbers',[2] thereby reinstating the Pythagoreans in full force. Pythagoreanism aside, one is reminded of the Democritean universe, which, while consisting of atoms and void, rests on two fundamental principles above all, namely the full and the empty. But 'full' and 'empty' being in the first instance mere adjectives, however much Democritus reifies them through the trope of nominalization, one must inevitably ask precisely what the items are that are presumed to be full and empty. Regions they can only be, over

---

[2] L. E. Hahn and P. A. Schilpp, eds., *The Philosophy of W. V. Quine* (La Salle, Ill.: Open Court, 1986), pp. 402, 516.

which alone (it is at least arguable) Democritus is engaged in quantifying; and in Quine's case as well, it is not as if there were two sorts of objects: namely, his gerrymandered space-time regions and their quantitative states. For the latter prove to be merely 'adjectival'—that is, predicative on the former. Appealing now to the 'equivalence' of regional and punctual ontologies, our nihilist will refuse to believe that merely by eliminating each of Quine's regions in favour of the set of points lying within it, one could be supposed to exchange a true ontology for a false one. Equally 'adequate to the facts', as one says informally, for facts as such are conspicuously absent from both, the two ontologies—one regional, the other punctual—are admitted to be logically incompatible. If they happen to agree as to the truth of '$(\exists x)$ x is a set', that is the merest accident, for a third ontology can be constructed (punctual or regional, as you prefer) in which, in line with a suggestion of von Neumann, functions are pressed into service in order to replace sets. To be, then, is always to exist relative to this or that valid conceptual scheme or, in Nelson Goodman's splendid phrase, 'way of world-making', since, on the present view, nothing whatever can be allowed to exist in itself, absolutely speaking. If on the contemporary scene it is Goodman who probably comes closest to filling the role of nihilist, his performance is flawed at the moment that he steps out of character to insist that there are no sets, not merely relative to this or that way of worldmaking, but absolutely speaking, sets being for him the merest figments of mathematical 'hanky-panky'. Entitled to deny outright the existence of F's, the nihilist is even obliged to do so in respect to certain values of F—for example, 'mermaid'. When it comes to sets, however, especially for one like Goodman who prides himself on his overtly 'constructional' approach to worldmaking, they ought to be recognized as on a par with mountains as emergent entities.

In the quarrel between realist and anti-realist, if the task of the one, according to Michael Dummett, lies in rendering the defence of his position 'convincing', that of the other consists in showing his own position to be 'coherent'. This issue of internal coherence arises specifically with regard to the ontological status of those very ways of worldmaking relative to some of which 'the pain in my foot' (to choose but one example) will succeed in denoting an object, even while relative to others it can only play a pragmatic role. Abstract entities on the face of it, the ways of worldmaking are required by systematic considerations alone to exist in themselves, absolutely speaking, for it is only relative to one or more of them that anything else can partake of such limited existence as is left over. Regardless of whether or not this difficulty can be overcome, there is one influential argument for realism from which I am eager to distance myself. Associated with the name of Tarski, who was found in Chapter 5 to pose the gravest challenge to our entire undertaking, his famous T-sentences are widely held today, ironically enough, to provide the means for pulling the metaphysical rabbit of realism out of the linguistic hat. Precisely by conjuring with T-sentences like (10), our semantic realists proceed to exorcise the spell of anti-realism.

(10) The English sentence 'There are regions each of which is composed of infinitely many points' is true if and only if there are regions each of which is composed of infinitely many points.

(11) There are regions each of which is composed of infinitely many points.

Embedded twice over in (10), (11) figures there once with and once without quotation marks, and any doubts as to whether there is an objective reality to which at least some of our sentences, the true ones, can be expected to correspond, (10) is designed to allay in the most semantically vivid fashion. The trouble, of course, is that our nihilist will insist that if (11) is true relative to some of the viable ways of worldmaking, it is certainly false relative to others, notably those like our regional and punctual ontologies that play favourites as between regions and points. And that can only mean that, worldbreaker as well as worldmaker, he refuses to acknowledge an objective reality to which (if we are lucky) sentences like (11) can semantically succeed in corresponding. Moreover, he is now found even to reject (10), for (10) can be true only under two conditions: namely, if (11) is true *simpliciter* or if (11) is false *simpliciter*. Taken informally, (10) might be supposed to be true even for the anti-realist until it is realized that, technically, the T-sentence of (11) is supplied only by (12):

(12)   [The English sentence '(11)' is true $\supset$ (11)] $\cdot$ [(11) $\supset$ the English sentence '(11)' is true.]

And here the semantics of any sentence with the form 'p $\supset$ q' (let alone any with the form 'p $\supset$ q $\cdot$ q $\supset$ p') simply stipulates that the non-standard, relativistic assignment of truth values in which our nihilist indulges cannot be tolerated. Committed, one might say, to a non-standard semantics for sentences like (10), the anti-realist has resources of his own to draw on.

24

Love

The radical anti-realist will accept no statement (that logically entails one) of the form 'There are F's' as being literally true as it stands, though he is often prepared to assent to such statements provided he can understand himself to be indulging in the rhetorical trope of reification when he does so. Cherished above all by the poet, all such tropes involved in the non-literal use of language lie within the scope of poetics as broadly conceived, and the philosopher is thus seen to be engaged in poetics whenever, as a local anti-realist, he is found to be only nominally committed to points, mountains, sensations, numbers, or whatever. That poetry proper should emerge, ultimately, as positively thematic for the metaphysician, one has every right to expect, quite apart from the following consideration. Despite all Plato's efforts, if the question were posed in classical antiquity, 'Where is wisdom the more likely to be found, in the pages of an Aristotle or in those of a Sophocles?', one can only fear that it is the poet, not the philosopher, who would prevail in almost any forum of informed opinion. Nor is it to be supposed that a questionnaire circulated today would issue in results more flattering to the philosopher. As to how one might go about investigating the putative wisdom of the poets, the philosopher finds himself very much at a loss, though it may be supposed that Plato will have to be consulted as an inevitable resource, being arguably in his own right a great poet as well as a great philosopher.

One text in particular stands out, Aristophanes' speech in the *Symposium*, for it is there above all that the wisdom of the poet, assuming there to be any such thing, is convincingly displayed to us. Almost too successfully, however, for the philosopher can hardly be expected to ask whether it is literally true that prelapsarian man, being then round all over, with two faces looking in opposite directions, and whirling along with four arms and four legs like an acrobat, was subsequently sliced down the middle for his defiance of the gods. In its own way a superb exercise in theory-building, the myth is designed to explain the following obscure fact about those who are in love. Venery aside, 'they cannot even say what they would have of one another,' for 'the soul of each is wishing for something that it cannot express, only divining and darkly hinting what it wishes' (192c–d in the Loeb translation). It turns out, however, if only with the help of the poet, that this inarticulate longing allows of being expressed by way of a good approximation: the lovers wish 'from being two to become one' (192e3), as they were in pre-lapsarian times, before each was divided from his other half. Conceding at once that the poet is addressing us on a peculiarly intimate level, the philosopher characteristically protests that it is only when we leave the hard, logico-metaphysical core of philosophy and range out into the softer, more humanistic periphery that the one undertaking has very much bearing on the other. Love in particular would appear to be so much the special preserve of the poet that the metaphysician is disqualified here from the outset.

Waiving all mythology, there is some reason to believe that lovers do in fact wish from being two to become one, and as we are inevitably addicted to the literal, I cannot refrain from urging that the Aristophanic hypothesis to the effect that the greater their love, the more do lovers yearn to be one be tested against the empirical facts by some imaginative team of social psychologists specializing perhaps in the sociology of small groups. Methodological issues regarding experimental design being by no means routine in the present instance, I fear that the greatest obstacle to my proposal may lie rather in the antecedent conviction that a scientific hypothesis could never be identical with a poetic conceit. Beyond the empirical issue and of still keener interest to us must of course be the conceptual one of clarifying what it is that becoming one might consist in for our lovers. That they can only 'divine' what they would have of one another suggests that even 'becoming one' may serve as scarcely more than a place-holder for what needs to be filled in with the proper content. Suppose, then, that I make a thematic suggestion of my own. At a minimum, becoming one for our lovers consists in their jointly constituting a single entity, seeing that the '*x* is a constituent of *y*' relation will be recalled from Chapter 17 as second only to the identity relation itself when it comes to metaphysical first principles. One is inevitably unnerved, then, to find Democritus insisting, with Aristotle's approval, that 'one thing cannot be made out of two nor two out of one'. An eliminative materialist of the most radical sort, Democritus appears to rule out from his austere ontology all so-called emergent entities—even mountains and rivers—on the ground that two or more entities can never combine to produce a new one. Arguably an anti-realist about mountains, he would presumably be prepared to assert in Mackie's idiom that 'mountain statements, though not themselves true, are surrogates for clusters of statements about atoms that can be true'.

Precisely what single entity our Aristophanic lovers may be expected to constitute emerges now as a further puzzle in its own right, for if the pairing axiom of set theory assures us that they cannot fail to constitute a doubleton set, it is scarcely to be supposed that the fulfilment of their deepest desire will be found therein. Although grounds for selectively doubting the pairing axiom are available, as when one considers the so-called proper classes of von Neumann—for example, the class not set of all sets that are not members of themselves—which are 'too large' to be admitted as members of any set or class on pain of Russell's paradox, we can certainly insist that neither of our lovers is identical with any such proper class. The heavy physicality of the Aristophanic myth suggests in any case that it will not satisfy our lovers merely to constitute some abstract, Platonic entity. No mere Platonic lovers, they. Looking then for a concrete alternative, the philosopher will consult at once the sum-individuals or so-called fusions of mereology, which appear to be operative in the poet's account as well when the god Hephaestus with his 'instruments' proposes to the lovers that he is 'ready to fuse and weld you together in a single piece', drawing on the words that the Loeb translator somewhat freely puts into his mouth. The fusions of logician and poet alike being seen here to be only metaphorical, there is this difference between them. If the fusions of mereology characteristically fall short of literal fusion, as when two strips of metal are fused end to end, the literal fusing back to back or even front to front of our lovers—let them then be joined like Siamese twins—as undertaken by the metallurgical god can only be regarded as a grotesque caricature of their hearts' desire.

What sort of ultra-fusion might then be expected to satisfy them? Turning now from one poet to another, Spenser's conceit in the Mutability Cantos regarding two Irish rivers: namely, the nymph Molanna—that is, the Behanna river—and her beloved, the Fanchin—that is, the Funsheon—can hardly fail to provide a gratifying model.

> So now her waves pass through the pleasant plain
> Till with the Fanchin she herself do wed,
> And (both combined) themselves in one fair river spread.[1]

It may thus be supposed that if lovers were rivers, only then would their prospects for truly uniting and becoming one be at all bright; but that subjunctive, contrary-to-fact conditional can only suggest that the comic mode of the Aristophanic myth disguises a tragic vision, which rules out any metaphysical consummation of the erotic. The tragedy is of the essence. Let it even be allowed, in the spirit of accidentalism, if not ultra-Scotism, that there may be a possible world where human beings metamorphose into rivers, preserving their identity, rather as caterpillars metamorphose into butterflies. That would not suffice. If our lovers are to achieve their bliss, they must fuse as sentient rivers, and it is thus no accident that the poet is found to be projecting a presumably impossible state of affairs in which a river and a nymph are identical with one another.

Beyond even the 'constitution' relation, the deeper one of identity is seen to undergo a crisis when the Aristophanic myth comes in effect to be reactivated in our own time by Bernard Williams who, by posing the issue afresh, has given rise to extended discussion regarding the diachronic identity of persons where the terms 'fusion' and especially 'fission' figure as routine jargon.[2] Projecting a case where, in effect, a human being undergoes fission

[1] Spenser, *Faerie Queene*, VII. vi. 53.
[2] B. Willimas, *Problems of the Self* (Cambridge: Cambridge University Press, 1973).

like an amoeba, Williams imagines a man being sliced down the middle (cf. Plato, *Symposium*, 190d5–8); with each part regenerating, two persons are shortly to be seen, each of whom in the absence of the other one would suppose to be (identical with) the original man. Of the 'three'—call them 'Tom', 'Dick', and 'Harry'—though it is evident that Dick is distinct from Harry, Arthur Prior has dared to suggest[3] that maybe it could be allowed by us both that Dick = Tom and that Harry = Tom. When so sober a logician as Prior dares to tamper with the transitivity of identity, which entails that if Dick = Tom and Tom = Harry, then Dick = Harry, we have grounds for supposing that our lovers— love in any case has often been felt to be irrational—may well be hankering for the very same thing. Does not Prior's suggestion, albeit in reverse, define exactly the intentional object of their desire, namely to fuse together into a single entity with which each will be identical (leaving it open perhaps whether they will then be identical with one another)? That pretty much seems to be Aristotle's view at *Politics*, 2. 1. 1262b12–15, when in making a somewhat different, though closely related, point he says that if *per impossibile* our lovers from being two are to become one, 'it is necessary that both perish or one of them anyway'. Maybe then the suicides of Romeo and Juliet are to be regarded as the poetic expression of a metaphysical necessity.

The only alternative account must presumably go somewhat as follows, reverting now to Spenser's rivers. Instead of ceasing to exist, à la Aristotle, beyond the point at which they fuse, they may be supposed to persist, but not as rivers, for it is not simply to be assumed that every river is necessarily a river in the *de re* sense. On fusing, then, let them continue to exist not as rivers but as discernibly different currents of water that jointly constitute a third river. Although that is probably one way in which the locution 'two becoming one' may be assigned a semantics—that is, truth conditions—I cannot believe that the yearnings of lovers could be assuaged by any such mere side-by-side-ness. Let us then postulate that when the rivers fuse, their waters lose their individuality by totally intermingling. If here at last the heart's desire

---

[3] A. Prior, 'Opposite Number', *Review of Metaphysics, 1957–1958*, pp. 463–88.

is convincingly represented, I fear that again we are envisioning a logically impossible state of affairs. Taken literally, loss of one's individuality can only mean loss of one's haecceity, and that entails ceasing to exist. Furthermore, it is to be noticed that it is not the rivers themselves that are said to lose their individuality, but their waters; as for the two quantities of water, however much they may intermingle physically, they must remain logically distinct to the end as scattered objects. Although Milton's angels 'embrace' in a fashion 'easier than air with air' when 'total they mix', one can only share Adam's puzzlement as to how exactly, in their love life, they 'mix irradiance', seeing that this 'union of pure with pure desiring' must somehow eschew the 'obstacle[s]' that arise not only if 'flesh' is to 'mix with flesh' but even if soul is to mix with soul,[4] for it is not to be supposed that shifting from body to soul can remedy matters when it comes to the metaphysical obstacle enshrined in the Kripkean necessity of diversity, according to which if x and y are distinct in one possible world (say, the actual one), they will also be so in every possible world. An impossible world it must then be that lovers in their desperate passion wish to actualize.

My erotic pessimism can probably be overcome only on the basis of a more or less radical rejection of one's characteristic realism, where one simply assumes that reality consists of crisp, discrete objects. Suppose now that as an anti-realist one rejects any such determinate domain of objects. Less radically, for one reason or another (perhaps owing to some form of eliminative materialism—for example, Quine's if not Democritus's), one may simply decline in one's ontology to quantify over persons as such. In either case, whether as an anti-realist *tout court* or merely as an anti-realist regarding persons, the putative yearning of lovers to become one will be subjected to a rational reconstruction that, if it does not dissolve the problem at the outset, may be expected to allow a happy resolution of it. If our lovers were never really two in the first place, nothing can stand in the way of their fusion. Realist and anti-realist can thus agree that in threatening to undermine one's (putative) identity, love is charged with the deepest metaphysical import. How that might be

---

[4] Milton, *Paradise Lost*, viii. 614–29.

expressed in a cycle of poems remains the task of some future poet. The poet is not the only one who stands to gain. The philosopher stands to gain still more from this association—I dare not say fusion—of philosophy and poetry, particularly at a time when it has come to be felt (the words are Richard Rorty's) that the philosopher is no longer 'entitled . . . to take credit for being wise as well as clever'. In fact, any suggestion that 'wise' might be predicated of his researches leaves the analytical philosopher feeling distinctly uneasy, though he has come to feel altogether at home with metaphysics, and it is not to be doubted (sticking to surface diction) that the words 'metaphysics' and 'wisdom' gravitate to one another.

The source of the unease can be traced back to Aristotle himself, who at the point where he even defines metaphysics by identifying it with wisdom finds himself obliged to qualify his identity thesis. There is practical as well as theoretical wisdom, and metaphysics can be identified only with the latter. It is thus to be surmised that wisdom *sans phrase* can be predicated only where at least some practical guidance as to the conduct of life is forthcoming. Thanks to my having shown in effect how and why it is that metaphysicians make the best lovers, even the most technical studies in abstract ontology can now be recognized as never ceasing to hover in the neighbourhood of wisdom. If erotic wisdom in particular presupposes some understanding of what the prospects might be of our lovers succeeding in becoming at any rate psychologically one, Aristotle has already indicated where we are to turn; namely, to Plato, *Republic*, v. 462d, where the theme is explored in specifically political terms.

Afterword

Virtually anticipating the French Revolution, Kant in his preface to the second edition of the *Critique of Pure Reason* indicates that his programme is designed to 'prevent the scandal which sooner or later is sure to break out among the masses, as the result of the disputes to which metaphysicians (and, as such, finally also the clergy) inevitably become involved'. That the fate of nations might actually depend, if only indirectly, on the rarefied disputes of metaphysicians, as they drift down into the Republic of Letters, remains a conviction on the continent of Europe that has not been altogether extinguished even in our time. However, in the English-speaking world (looking no further), all such alarums and excursions can seem very remote indeed, and it may be readily supposed that none of the discussions in the present volume—waiving Chapter 23, which features the spectre of nihilism—is liable to inspire a metaphysical terrorist, like Robespierre, to shake the foundations of civil society.

The sober emphasis on logic might well appear to provide all the assurance that anyone could desire. For if philosophy as a whole may be conceded to be one of the humanities, there is yet one branch of philosophy which, after Frege though not a moment before, the *annus mirabilis* being 1879, qualifies (anomalously enough) as one of the sciences proper, and it is not to be doubted that the Fregean revolution in logic, taken quite by itself, must be recognized as one of the great moments in the history of philosophy. That it can also be seen in retrospect to have inaugurated the renewal of classical metaphysics, I take to have been fully established in these pages, though it must be confessed to be among the best-kept secrets of our time. One is inclined rather to suppose, with a humanist like Allan Bloom, that if philosophy 'has a scientific component, logic, which is attached to the sciences', it 'could easily be detached from philosophy', for, as 'practiced by competent specialists', it 'responds to none of the permanent philosophic questions'. *How* responsive to the permanent questions, as defined by Plato, Aristotle, and Kant, logic has proved to be in the hands of such 'specialists' as Frege, Quine, and Kripke, I have been at the greatest pains to document. Most evident when logic is taken to be involved in set theory where Plato flourishes, this responsiveness was never so exquisite as in Quine's prophetic statement that 'reversion to Aristotelian essentialism . . . is required if quantification into modal contexts is to be insisted on'. More narrowly conceived, however, as a purely formal discipline, logic may even yet be felt to be a mere organon or instrument of philosophy, rather than a proper part of it, and it was in fact not long after Aristotle's death that this view of logic as organon acquired currency.

Distinguishing the form from the content of a statement, one says that the (logical) form of 'All men are mortal' is 'Every F is a G', featuring above all the logical word 'every'; whereas the content of the statement is supplied by the predicates 'x is a man' and 'x is mortal'. Mere use of the logical or formal words alone— 'and', 'not', 'either/or', 'neither/nor', 'if-then', 'all', and 'some'—can never suffice to build a sentence, since extra-logical or extra-formal words in the form of predicates are always required to supply content. That at any rate is the basic thought of logic as such. Critical now proves to be the anomalous role of identity in first-order predicate logic, for once ' = ' or '$x = y$' is conceded to be a logical expression (it is of course a predicate), logical words do suffice for building whole sentences, some false, others true, as '$(x)(y) x = y$' and '$(\exists x)(\exists y) \sim (x = y)$' demonstrate. If a powerful case can thus be made in support of the thesis that logic proper is just first-order predicate logic *without* identity, the sheer mechanics of his science renders any such purist approach singularly unattractive to the logician. After noticing that any statement of the form '$(\exists x)(\exists y) x$ is an $F \cdot y$ is an $F \cdot x$ is a G $\cdot \sim (y$ is a $G)$' commits one to the existence of *at least* two F's, the logician casts about for a way of guaranteeing a commitment to exactly two. Identity comes into play here, as one adds this: 'and for any z if z is an F then $z = x$ or $z = y$'. How implausible, then, to take 'at least two' as belonging to logic and 'exactly two' as lying outside! So identity does belong to logic after all? In their more candid moments most logicians today are probably prepared to allow that there may be no answer to the question, seeing that the case *against* the hypothesis arguably balances the case *for* the hypothesis. Call this clash 'the Hegelian Antinomy', for it was Hegel who thematically insisted that the very thought of logic as a purely formal, antonomous enterprise that abstracts from all content can be shown to be inherently unstable.

If metaphysics emerges now with the recognition of that instability, the quasi-logical Principle of Identity comes to pose a challenge of its own. Although every substance (Aristotle) or every object (Frege) will be allowed to be self-identical, Frege shares Aristotle's qualms as to the propriety of saying that everything *sans phrase* is identical with itself. It is not merely the universal quantifier 'every' or 'everything' that is felt to be unstable. When we say, 'There is something that Socrates and Plato both are, namely wise,' the sentence fragment 'there is something' functions in a *pros hen* (Aristotle) or second-order (Frege) fashion. Dispensing with all such destabilizing locutions, one may choose to paraphrase them crisply away by saying, 'There is something that Socrates and Plato both *have*, namely wisdom.' But that statement in its turn may be felt to involve an unstable idiom, as the nominalist at any rate glosses it as merely saying in effect that Socrates and Plato are both wise.

If the traditional nominalist convicts the utterance of being infected with the rhetorical trope of reification, it is only in recent years that we have come to recognize that pretty much the same sort of anti-realist strategy can be applied across the board to such utterances as 'There is a pain in my foot,' or 'There is a cat on the mat,' since pains and cats alike prove to be as problematical as wisdom itself when it comes to quantifying over them —that is to say, reifying them—in one's ontology. Cats in particular being recognized as emergent entities that supervene on the molecules that compose them, the purest sort of emergent object was found in the mathematician's sets where the ZF intuition serves as a first approximation of a metaphysical insight.

When Homer reifies the anger of Achilles in the first line of the *Iliad*, poet and metaphysician are seen to come within hailing distance of each other; and it is precisely this joint affinity of poetry and mathematics to the metaphysical enterprise that I have especially enjoyed cultivating in these pages. Mere doctrine is not enough. Platonism, essentialism, materialism, and anti-realism: these four metaphysical doctrines bulk largest in contemporary discussions, and I have laboured to exhibit them within a framework constituted by Aristotle's conception of ontology as the theory of being as such. Underlying these discussions, it is 'No entity without identity' that expresses for the contemporary philosopher the principle *par excellence* of being *qua* being, though he will inevitably be disconcerted when I insist that the maxim plays a synthetic a priori role in his thinking.

Conducted in the immediate neighbourhood of logic, these dry discussions are widely believed—not least by the professional philosopher himself—to bear only the most tenuous relation to wisdom. Hence the urgent need to pursue them in close conjunction with mathematics and poetry, seeing that the one lies at the core of the sciences and the other at the heart of the humanities. More than any putative world-view encompassing the two, it is the cultivation of metaphysical connoisseurship regarding mathematics and poetry that offers the best prospect today of achieving a reasonable facsimile of wisdom.

Glossary of Logical Symbols

x	'or'
~	'not'
·	'and'
⊃	'if . . . then'
=	'is identical with'
∈	'is a member of'
□	'it is necessary that' (but see p. 151)
◇	'it is possible that' (but see p. 154)
(∃x) or (Σx)	'there exists an x' (or 'something is')
(x) or (∀x)	'every x' (or 'everything')
(∃F)	'there exists a property F' (but see p. 164)
(F)	'every property F' (but see p. 164)
f(x)	'the mathematical function f' (it is read as 'f of x')

Index

Index compiled by Peva Keane

OXFORD

MORE OXFORD PAPERBACKS

Details of a selection of other books follow. A complete list of Oxford Paperbacks, including The World's Classics, Twentieth-Century Classics, OPUS, Past Masters, Oxford Authors, Oxford Shakespeare, and Oxford Paperback Reference, is available in the UK from the General Publicity Department, Oxford University Press (JN), Walton Street, Oxford OX2 6DP.

In the USA, complete lists are available from the Paperbacks Marketing Manager, Oxford University Press, 200 Madison Avenue, New York, NY 10016.

Oxford Paperbacks are available from all good bookshops. In case of difficulty, customers in the UK can order direct from Oxford University Press Bookshop, 116 High Street, Oxford, Freepost, OX1 4BR, enclosing full payment. Please add 10 per cent of published price for postage and packing.

THE PROBLEMS OF PHILOSOPHY

Bertrand Russell

First published in 1912, this classic introduction to the subject of philosophical inquiry has proved invaluable to the formal student and general reader alike. It has Russell's views succinctly stated on material reality and idealism, knowledge by acquaintance and by description, induction, knowledge of general principles and of universals, intuitive knowledge, truth and falsehood, the distinctions between knowledge, error, and probable opinion, and the limits and the value of philosophical knowledge.

A foreword Russell wrote in 1924 for a German translation has been added as an appendix. Here Russell gave details of how some of his views had changed since *The Problems of Philosophy* was written.

An OPUS book

ETHICS SINCE 1900

Mary Warnock

'In this lively and fascinating book Mrs Warnock tells with admirable clarity the story of the development of English moral philosophy in the twentieth century . . . most attractively written, spontaneous, forthright and unfuzzy.' *Times Literary Supplement*

'The book is a classic among handbooks: unpretentious, but very individual, with a vigour and clarity which make it as attractive to read as it is instructive.' *Christian World*

AESTHETICS

Anne Sheppard

Can we sensibly talk of 'meaning' and 'truth' in relation to works of art? Is knowledge of the artist's intention relevant to one's appreciation of the work? Should moral considerations enter into criticism of the arts?

In this introduction to aesthetics Anne Sheppard tackles the profoundly complex questions that lie at the heart of the subject. She describes various different theories of what it is that all works of art share that gives them their value, combining brief accounts of historically influential views with an explanation of the philosophical issues raised. While all art forms are discussed, a particular emphasis on literature serves to illustrate some of these issues in sharper detail: the concepts of truth and meaning, critical interpretation and evaluation, the way in which art can inculcate values and attitudes, and the relationship between art and morals. In drawing all these threads together Anne Sheppard analysis the sort of aesthetic judgements we make when we examine a painting, look at a building, listen to a piece of music, or study a work of literature.

GAIA

A New Look at Life on Earth

J. E. Lovelock

Dr Lovelock's Gaia hypothesis first took the scientific world by storm in the mid-seventies. He proposed that all living things on the earth are part of a giant organism, involving air, oceans, and land surface, which for millions of years has controlled the conditions needed for a healthy planet. While stressing the need for continued vigilance, Dr Lovelock argues that, thanks to Gaia, our fears of pollution-extermination may be unfounded.

'This is the most fascinating book that I have read for a long time.' Kenneth Mellanby in the *New Scientist*

FREE WILL AND RESPONSIBILITY

Jennifer Trusted

'Jennifer Trusted's aim in *Free Will and Responsibility* is to introduce the stubborn problem of free will to beginners in philosophy and at the same time to make some contribution of her own to its solution. She writes lucidly, displays a wide acquaintance with the relevant literature, from Aristotle onwards, and packs a great deal of argument and exposition into a relatively small compass.' A. J. Ayer, *New Humanist*

'a determined, methodical onslaught on one of the classical, most familiar problems—or entanglement of problems—of philosophy since its earliest days . . . the well-trodden ground is clearly and sensibly traced out, and the readers for whom it is intended should indeed be helped by it—which is no mean achievement.' G. J. Warnock, *Expository Times*

MORAL PHILOSOPHY

D. D. Raphael

Do moral philosophers have anything to say which is useful, let alone comprehensible, to people with more down-to-earth concerns? Professor Raphael would answer 'Yes' on both counts. Unlike most 'introductions' to moral philosophy, this book is written expressly for the beginner. Also, it is not confined to the theory of ethics in any narrow sense, but makes a point of showing the connections between abstract ethics and practical problems.

'It would be difficult to find a clearer introduction to modern moral philosophy.' *Tablet*

An OPUS book